How and Why We Make Games

This book delves into the intricate realms of games and their creation, examining them through cultural, systemic, and, most notably, human lenses. It explores diverse themes such as authorship, creative responsibility, the tension between games as a product and games as a form of cultural expression, and the myth of a universal audience.

This book analyzes why we should put politics in our games and how hyperrealism may be a trap. It also proposes a new framework for thinking about game narrative and a different paradigm for the production altogether. Topics tackled are approached from a multidisciplinary perspective, so be prepared to read both about Peter Paul Rubens and John Carmack. There are also graphs, system rhetorics discussions, and the market reality—stakeholders, return on investments, and the gaming bubble bursting.

This book is written for readers passionate about the craft of making games, including journalists and industry professionals. It offers a more humanistic perspective on games, presented by experienced writers who know the intricacies of game development.

How and Why We Make Games
The Creative Confusion

Written by
Marta Fijak
Artur Ganszyniec

CRC Press
Taylor & Francis Group
Boca Raton London New York

CRC Press is an imprint of the
Taylor & Francis Group, an **informa** business

First edition published 2025
by CRC Press
2385 NW Executive Center Drive, Suite 320, Boca Raton FL 33431

and by CRC Press
4 Park Square, Milton Park, Abingdon, Oxon, OX14 4RN

CRC Press is an imprint of Taylor & Francis Group, LLC

© 2025 Marta Fijak and Artur Ganszyniec

ISBN: 978-1-032-35045-5 (hbk)
ISBN: 978-1-032-34332-7 (pbk)
ISBN: 978-1-003-32503-1 (ebk)

DOI: 10.1201/9781003325031

Typeset in Caslon
by MPS Limited, Dehradun

To our wives, Joannas.

Contents

Author biographies

Marta Fijak has been making games since 2013. With a master's degree in experimental biology and an engineering degree in computer science, she decided to dedicate her life to games instead. She tried every form of game development, from basement indie with 20 players to a BAFTA-nominated game with ~2 million players, to F2P with ~10 million players. She has been a gameplay programmer, system and technical designer, and eventually a lead designer and a creative director. Recently, and not under NDA, she worked (a lot) on *Frostpunk* and (a little) on *Rimworld*. She teaches game design at the Warsaw Film School, consults on games, and, just in general, can not shut up about them.

Artur Ganszyniec has been making games since 2006. He is a data analyst by education, storyteller by choice, designer by trade, and autistic by birth. He has worked on AAA games, overseeing the story for the first two *The Witcher* games, ethical mobile F2P games, and artistic indie darlings. He teaches game design at the Lodz University of Technology, consults on games, and works for the Polish game industry as a part of the Polish Gamedev Workers Union.

1

GAMES AS A MEDIUM

ARTUR GANSZYNIEC

Video games were born in the late 1950s/early 1960s, so as early as there were video displays to display the game on, computers that could calculate what to display, and (last but not least) people who felt the need to use their serious, room-spanning machines to make games. This probably says something important about our species.

Spacewar!, developed by students of Massachusetts Institute of Technology in 1962, is probably the first video game played on multiple computer installations. And, because people generally like to play with what they play, it was heavily modded by the users. Nothing new under the sun.

The commercial history of video games started in the 1970s with the release of *Magnavox Odyssey,* the first home video game console. Others followed with classic arcade video games such as *Computer Space* and *Pong.* The latter holds an important place in my personal history of games.

My first encounter with video games happened in the late 1980s in still-communist Poland, when my parents managed to *fix* a second-hand color TV smuggled from West Germany through an extended network of family and friends. With it came a pair of strange controllers, and a dark gray box that you could plug into the said TV. And on the gray box, there was a clone of *Pong.*

So, when in the wide Western world the video game market swelled after the arrival of the first ROM cartridge-based home consoles, flourished with arcade games such as *Pac-Man* or *Space Invaders,* and then crashed flooded by too many, too derivative products, I was learning how to beat my sister in a game of ping-pong played on our home television.

DOI: 10.1201/9781003325031-1

There are many great publications focused solely on the history of video games, so I won't reiterate all important points of development here. Let me just sketch a rough timeline, with ten games that are to be considered for preservation by the Library of Congress. This so-called *game canon* highlights games that started new genres, still significant in the industry. These games are as follows: *Spacewar!*—a 1962 space combat video game; *Star Raiders*—a 1980 space combat video game; *Zork*—a 1977 text-based adventure video game; *Tetris*—a 1985 puzzle video game; *SimCity*—a 1989 city-building simulation video game; *Super Mario Bros 3*—a 1988 platform game; *Civilization I/II*—a 1991, and 1996 for Civ II, turn-based strategy 4X video game; *Doom*—a 1993 first-person shooter; *Warcraft* series—a series of real-time strategy (RTS) games that began in 1994; and *Sensible World of Soccer*—a 1994 football video game.

The recognition and, as *The New York Times* put it, "an assertion that digital games have a cultural significance and a historical significance" came over a half-century after *Spacewar!* was created in 2006. Up to that point, video games were mostly perceived as toys, a pastime suited for children and adolescents.

During my youth, playing video games was something that was happening among children—and the occasional *hip* adults, who introduced new technologies brought from the West. I grew up in a small town in post-communist Poland, so your experience may vary. But even in my youth, it was a vibrant culture, even with a slightly homemade, post-apocalyptic vibe. Most of the hardware was second-hand and sent back from the West (Germany or the USA, depending on where your industrious family members emigrated) and the games were copied over and over on magnetic audio cassettes. When they were loading, you had to sit still and quiet, because even the slightest tremor of the floor could result in the game not loading properly. I still remember the feeling of holding my breath and listening to the weird electronic noises of the cassette, wondering what game would load and if we would find out how to play it. Most of the cassettes were unnamed, and most of the games were in English, a language we didn't know.

I think that I saw my first original game when I was in high school. The funny thing is that the games I played as a child, although for sure not original, were not *technically* pirated. There were no software copyright laws in Poland at that time, and with no laws, there could be no crime.

Apart from home consoles, there were video game arcades. I remember the best the one in a seaside town, where we used to spend our family holidays. We would pool our allowances with other kids, and spend the money playing games. The one I remember the most was *Golden Axe* which we would play in pairs, one of us controlling the movement and the other pressing the attack buttons. The games were expensive and we wanted to squeeze the most value from our money.

There were also handheld consoles, but only the most fortunate managed to get one. Our family treasure was an old GameBoy with a single cartridge of a *Mario* game. It was the only GameBoy in the area, so for a long time I had no idea that, out there, were other cartridges with other games.

There were a lot of video games in my youth, and they were both fascinating and mysterious. They were also a children's thing. The parents did not understand or care for the games, and they fell into the wide category of "do not sit so long in front of the TV, go outside and play!" At least, such was my experience. But from what I gathered, many shared similar stories.

When I was at the university, the situation normalized. We had PCs, with original games on CDs waiting to be bought, many of which were fully localized to Polish. There were video game magazines. But the general perception did not change much. Games were a waste of time, entertainment (if not toys), and something to be observed with suspicion. It was the late 1990s and the "video games cause violence" meme was circulating in the press and influenced the public understanding of the medium.

I graduated from the Warsaw School of Economics with a master's degree in data analysis and went to work in a big telecom company. Three years later, burnt out and disillusioned, I quit and started looking for a new gig. I decided to approach the problem with an open mind, so when a friend, whom I knew through our tabletop RPG sessions, reached out to me and said that they were looking for writers to work on a new video game, I gave it a try. The game was based on a series of books by my favorite Polish author, Andrzej Sapkowski, and was called *The Witcher*.

The interview went well and I got an offer, which I finally accepted. But for a few days, I was two minds about it. The project looked interesting, but it was a *video game*. Such a frivolous industry—I thought—not serious at all. Not real business, and, for sure, not art. I wanted to write, but for something that mattered. If not books, then at least movies. But I needed money, so I joined the team. And discovered, over the years, how wrong I was. Games turned out to be both a serious business and an important part of culture.

But in 2006 I saw it differently, as my worldview was shaped by the general understanding of the matter. Movies were serious, movies were art. But the games? They were none of those.

But in the late 1890s when movies as a medium were in their infancy, they were seen as a vulgar form of cheap entertainment for the working class, unsuited for telling coherent stories and arousing emotions other than a cheap thrill. It took movies a larger part of a century to grow from silent, black-and-white, two-minute documentary episodes about a train arriving at a station, or staged comedy sketches about the sprinkler sprinkled to the romantic classics like *Casablanca* or extravagant experiments like *Everything Everywhere All at Once*.

Movies left their infancy period behind. We know how to make a movie. We know how to write a script, how to sell it, how to plan a production, how to find the cast, how to shoot, how to edit, and how to post-process a movie. We know how to tell a feature movie from a short film, and a film etude. Particular methods change over time, with the changes in technology, but we've reached an understanding of what a movie is. The medium has matured.

In contrast to the movies, games are still going through their growing pains. The medium probably left its infancy period behind, but has it graduated from college yet? Or are we still in a cultural high school (if not a primary education)?

It doesn't help that video games are such a wide and varied field. What is a game? This is a question very similar to "What is a sport?" There are so many categories, genres, platforms, business models, etc. that even finding a practically useful level of abstraction when talking about our craft is a challenge. We still have no universal format for a design doc, not talking about a "script." We use many technologies, and every studio creates its own pipelines and best practices—only to change them when technology changes or too many of the employees rotate out of the project. Then again, we started later than the movies. Who knows where we will be in 70 years?

One may argue—and many indeed do—that some of the problems stem from the uniqueness of games as a medium. Games are interactive, can tell non-linear stories, the consumers are co-authors, etc. No wonder that in such an innovative, ever-changing, cutting-edge, one-and-only medium, we must constantly innovate. It is irrational to expect that we find one format to fit all the unique ways in which a concept of a *game* can be expressed.

But are games indeed so unique? I would argue that they are *specific*, such as opera is specific or ballet, experimental theater, or tabletop role-playing. They have their own needs, their means of expression, conventions, and know-how. They require a personalized approach, and tricks and formats that work in other media have to be adapted or replaced by ones more suited to this particular way of telling stories and providing experiences. But, in my opinion, there is nothing inherently *other* about video games as a medium. We can expect that in time, video game craft will develop and codify know-how and best practices that suit the specificity of the medium.

What is so specific about video games? First of all, they are games. Defining what a game is, is beyond the scope of this essay; there are many publications focused solely on this question. For a starting point for our deliberations, let's use the definition proposed by Kevin J. Maroney: "A game is a form of play with goals and structure." And from that stem features specific to the medium.

Of all the things that differentiate games from other media, the most important to me, as a designer, are participation, agency, and uncertainty. People who choose to play a game, as opposed to reading a book or binging *Netflix,* want to participate, to play an active role in what happens on the screen. They are, from the start, more invested in the medium, for good and for worse. On the one hand, they are more flexible when it comes to reasons to engage with the story or gameplay—when you *want* to play, almost any excuse is good enough. On the other hand, if they drop out of the game, their disappointment and resentment are deeper, because they have invested more. How many of us rage-quitted a book? And a game? There you are.

From the willingness to participate comes the need for agency. As a player, I am ready to be the driving force of the story, to cause change, and not only to experience it. Behavioral psychology defines people who have agency (agents) as goal-directed entities that are able to monitor their environment to select and perform efficient means-end actions that are available in a given situation to achieve an intended goal. And this is what I want to do when I play a game. I want to know my goals, understand my current situation, and have a range of tools or options that I can use to plan and execute my path toward the goal. To do that, I also need feedback about my previous actions that I can use to correct my course.

Any setup that gives me agency also breeds uncertainty. Games are no fun without a challenge, a mystery, a puzzle, and a chance to test oneself. The uncertainty can stem from the fact that I don't know the golden path or that I am not sure if I can perform all the actions needed to reach the goal. But the moment I understand what to do and am certain that I can do it, the game starts losing its allure. Unless, of course, there is a space for mastery and gaining pleasure from flawlessly performing a demanding task. However, not all games have a structure that can support mastery.

Taking all that into account, as a designer, I know that I must prepare a product that is to be *experienced* not just observed. And therein lies the specific nature of games as a medium. This shift of perspective affects how we tell stories and what stories can be told at all. It affects what tricks from other media we can use, from what we show and how (compare a traditional movie montage with camera work in First Person Perspective games), to what narrative tools work (*Heavy Rain* showed how hard it was to play the old unreliable narrator shtick in a game), to how we can present and execute the protagonist's dilemmas (as it is the player who will be in charge of the actual decision-making process). On top of that, there is a whole area of gameplay that simply does not exist in the more traditional media. One can argue that an author of a fantasy novel also has to balance the difficulty of boss fights versus the progression curve of the protagonist. But let's be honest, when you write a book the math is just not there, while when you design a game, the math is crucial.

Even the oldest trick in the books, *deus ex machina*, used in the context of a game has a distinctly different flavor than in an ancient tragedy. In the *machina* of a game, the player wants to be the *deus* and any god miraculously solving the protagonist's problems would be robbing the player of a hard-earned victory.

Although outsider tricks do not work, games are being made and are making an impact on players. Let's take a brief look at some video game-specific tools and approaches to choices, exploration, anticipation, immersion, reflection, and empathy.

From my perspective, in the heart of any good game, there is a set of interesting decisions. This concerns all layers of the game, from trying out gameplay tactics to planning exploration to deciding how to navigate a branching storyline, to choosing specific dialog options. To be effective and interesting, decisions in a game must steer away from two extremes. They must not be too random, and they must not present an optimal path. Both extremes kill the player's agency—I cannot make an informed choice if I can't predict results at all, and I feel compelled to choose an option that is clearly a "win." As Sid Meier said: "Given the opportunity, players will optimize the fun out of a game." And we, as creators, shouldn't give them such an opportunity.

This is a delicate balance to reach. I've seen many times (in my own games as well as in the projects I consulted or played) randomness sneaking up disguised as a surprise or plot twist. The optimal path, on the other hand, often interfered with the "morality" of a choice.

Most games have some kind of economy that is baked into the systems. So it is in real life, we need money, food, items, etc. to survive. At the same time, things that are important to us in real life, such as emotions, relationships, and our standing in society, translate poorly into the language of video games, unless backed up by a specific system. This creates an imbalance that calls for a specific design of choices. In a movie or a book, choosing personal wealth over being a decent human being is a classical dilemma. It makes Judas such a tragic and compelling character. In a game, things are different. Money has a systemic value that affects all aspects of the game, while "being decent" is just a flavor. I have a grim suspicion that in the privacy of their gaming dens, only the most hardcore roleplayers would not betray Jesus.

Reaching for a more grounded example, let's have a look at *This War of Mine,* a bleak survival game that simulates the life of civilians trapped in a destroyed city during a war. There were many moments in the game where you had to make a tough choice, e.g., rob an elderly couple of their possessions, which would increase your chances of survival, or let them be, hoping they will survive on their own. In most cases, it worked, as the context of a war was so extreme that being a decent human being in the face of almost certain death was a heroic choice. The players got that they were playing a tragedy, and survival at the cost of your soul was a bitter victory if a victory at all.

However, if you looked closer, you could notice that—for balance reasons—morally good choices, where you apparently resigned from a material reward, also rewarded you with resources, just in a delayed and indirect way. As soon as you noticed that the illusion shattered and a morally deep game became just a story-flavored resource manager. Don't get me wrong, *TWoM* was a good and important game. Yet, even the experienced team in 11 bit studios struggled with the systemic morality of player's choices.

Even if we put the morality of decisions aside, choices have another aspect that is interesting from a designer's and storyteller's perspectives. Choices tie in with the idea of exploration. Whether we are talking about choosing literal paths through three-dimensional game levels or mapping a path through a branching storyline, there is an important aspect of exploring to consider. I am talking about the freedom to look into every nook and cranny, the freedom to be lost and found, and the freedom to take stupid and irrational paths just for the fun of it. We all know how well the feeling of a lazy stroll through a familiar neighborhood translates into open-world games, and how satisfying getting from point A to point B can be, even if there is no challenge in it. On the contrary, we know how frustrating games can be when our exploration is hindered or turns out to be a scam. Moments that are cut out in most movies can make or break the experience of a game.

We explore when we believe in the game world, we are immersed in it and to plan our next steps we use our whole knowledge of the world, not just our understanding of the rules of that particular game. When we encounter an unexpected barrier that reminds us that "this is just a game," our immersion is broken and we are sad and disillusioned.

For many designers, game journalists, and players, immersion is the holy grail of games, the ultimate test proving if the product is any good. I get it. The feeling of being completely lost in a fictional world is precious and unique. And yet, from an author's perspective, there is another mind state that we want to induce sometimes, that stands in conflict with immersion. I am talking about reflection. When I'm immersed in the story world, I am the hero/ine and I act. My emotions, goals, and impulses are in sync with the needs of the protagonist and the story. But sometimes, we want the player to apply the moral of the story to their own life, to contrast the actions of the hero with the worldview of the person directing the hero, and to pose a question about how the consequences of the player's choices would translate to the real world. To do that, we need to snap the player of the reverie and give them space to reflect.

Sometimes, the moment of reflection comes at the very end of the game, like in *The Witness* which was a beautiful and mind-bending essay about how immersion rewires our brain. However, in most cases, we want the player to reflect at many points in the game and use their reflections to plan their next moves. We can't do that if the player is constantly immersed, especially in action-heavy games, when the adrenaline flows through the veins and shuts out not only reflection but also empathy. For every game, the immersion-to-reflection ratio may be different, but I will risk a thesis that a good game needs both elements.

Balancing systems and plot, decisions and context, and immersion and reflection, video games have the potential to become empathy machines. They can make you a protagonist of someone else's story, allow you to literally step in someone's shoes, make their decisions, and fight their struggles. To become someone else for a while, and then step back and reflect on the new, borrowed life experience. Becoming someone breeds familiarity and familiarity breeds empathy. I realize that it may sound idealistic and lofty, so I use a down-to-earth example to illustrate what I mean.

Horror movies are not my favorite genre, but I like and enjoy them. There is something cozy about being scared and repulsed in a controlled way while sitting under a blanket with a cup of tea. The only thing that bothers me, sometimes, is how stupid and reckless the protagonists are. Why are they splitting from the group? Why are they opening that door? Don't they realize there is a monster inside? And now it's too late! They are dead, and it's their own fault! Good riddance.

Then I played *Until Dawn*, an interactive drama horror video game by Supermassive Games. And guess what? I split from the party. I opened that door. I didn't realize there was a monster inside until it was too late. I was dead and it was my own fault! Good riddance.

I got so immersed that I forgot to reflect on what genre I was playing. I just knew that I was playing a game, and in a game, the protagonist wins. I got stupid and reckless, and killed a nice character. It was fun. It gave me empathy toward those doomed college kids in slashers. Their recklessness still bothers me, sometimes, but at least I deeply, viscerally *understand* what's happening. Because it happened to me too.

That was a fun example, but the tricks and tools I described are more than building blocks of *fun*. They are, above all, a means of expression for creators, a toolset an author can use to evoke certain emotions, put players in front of certain dilemmas, and present certain morals. To frame it differently: they are video game-specific stylistic tools that allow us to transcend the paradigm of *games as just toys*. In skilled hands, these tools allow games to be designed and constructed as commentary on emotions, events, and the state of the world—as works of culture.

There was never a lack of skilled hands and brilliant minds working on video games. So why did it take (is taking?) so long for the medium to be recognized as a valid and valuable part of our cultural landscape?

I think the disadvantage we had to face was that we had to build, at the same time, the products and the whole construction yard. Seventy years ago, no one knew what video games were and we had to figure it out in the only way possible—by making video games and reflecting on what was produced. Every medium needs a set of rules and conventions to act as the skeleton on which the actual body of work is done. Without such a foundation, every production needs to reinvent the wheel, and when you do that, sometimes you get a triangle and have to work around it. Which, as we all must admit, usually brings on suboptimal results. But how to start working on a set of tools and conventions for a new medium? I suppose, you do, what all great artists do: Steal.

Media share common DNA and some are more related than others. For centuries, opera stole tools and techniques from theater and vice versa, and when cinema came into existence, it started with actors and tools stolen from theater. And then, video games started drawing inspiration from cinema.

For years the most visible, quantifiable, and often the most praised indicator of the progress in the game industry has been graphics. With every new generation of GPU, memory chips, and ways of displaying pixels on the screen, the video part of video games has become more noticeable. If games were, as it seemed, going toward high visual fidelity, it was only natural to start mimicking tools from the craft that had already mastered the visual language produced for screen display—filmmaking.

When I entered the industry, in 2006, we all looked up to Hollywood as the most influential source of culturally impactful popular entertainment. "Cinematic" was the adjective that game developers strived for. We would discuss and dissect our favorite scenes from Tarantino or Eastwood movies. Our friends from more shooter-oriented companies had huge collections of movie clips as references for creating shoot-outs in any possible environment and circumstances. I would devour classical textbooks about screenwriting and storyboarding. We were learning, and with that, the industry was changing.

This fascination with Hollywood brought new ways of telling stories in games, but at the same time, created a way of working, where the good-looking parts were using a different language than the player-has-lots-to-do parts. Due to technical restrictions and, I suppose, lack of a new language, games at that time were made of literal *movies* (often pre-rendered or even full-motion video scenes with famous actors) submerged in interactive *games*. That allowed us to squeeze the most out of the software and hardware, and use all the sexy Hollywood tricks. It helped with the production as the movie parts and the game parts could, at least in theory, be produced independently from each other. But it also created a reality where the *watching* parts were not always in sync with the *playing* parts of the game when it came to the narrative, mood, or theme.

The situation also created a language where *story* and *gameplay* were seen as independent, usually opposing forces within the game. The tension and opposition were visible both during the production and in the final products.

Reflecting on such experiences, in his book *Video Game Storytelling*, Evan Skolnick wrote: "During the long slog of a game's dev cycle, it's frighteningly easy for 'Game Design plus Narrative' to become 'Game Design vs. Narrative.'" I would like to reflect for a moment on that sentence because it shows that even in 2014, very experienced gamedev professionals would not see the possibility that Narrative *was* Game Design (and vice versa). *Telling stories* in games was perceived as something fundamentally different than making the *actual game*. This perception is still alive and kicking.

Don't get me wrong, Hollywood and TV series are a great source of inspiration, and many of the tools games stole from their older siblings are very useful indeed. I just wish the umbilical cord had been severed earlier on, and that we created our own language and set of rules, specific to our medium.

When we look around, there are many other media that have elements similar to video games—experimental theater, comic books, live action role-playing games (LARPs), and poetry, to name only a few. They are not as well known and obvious as movies, and I guess it took people with a more general, less specialized education than programmers and gamers to spot potential inspirations.

Over the last few years, I have observed a steady stream of people from other branches of culture—journalists, people from theater, novelists, anthropologists, and psychologists—migrating to gamedev, and I think that our industry becomes richer with every such arrival.

There are also market forces at play. Some tools and techniques are consciously stolen from other media, but others develop and solidify organically because using them helps create good-selling games in a consistent way. And when a game sells well, the probability that the team will get to produce another, bigger game grows. And if they do, they probably use the techniques and tools that worked the last time. Survival of the fittest, one might say.

When we look at the game landscape, we will clearly see well-defined genres and sub-genres, some of them new, some in their prime, some already fading, some coming back from years in a coma.

We know how to consistently make those kinds of games; we have a set of rules and conventions that create a backbone of the productions and allow us to differentiate an RTS from a visual novel from a platformer.

At the same time, the bigger the games, the more expensive the production, and the more risk-averse the company becomes. There is only one small step from using well-tested tools to using *only* the tools that have been tested. There is a point, usually when a company enters the AAA space, when the rules and conventions of the genre, and the tools and techniques of the craft, stop acting as a skeleton supporting the growth of the medium. Instead, they become a carapace, and exoskeleton, supporting but also determining the shape and preventing growth.

Let's just look at the *Assassin's Creed* series by Ubisoft, which, after years of tentatively exploring the genre they created in 2007, folded onto itself and reset to the starting point in 2023, like a snake devouring its own tail.

To give credit, where credit is due, I fully appreciate what AAA and AA games did for our media. They built a foundation of recognizable genres, brought forth countless technological and organizational breakthroughs, pushed forward the language of UI and UX, etc. In my daily work, I have the privilege to use many of those improvements and they are the foundation for future games. After 70 years, we know how to make great, visually stunning, and engaging interactive entertainment, and earn good money doing that.

At the same time, my interest as a designer lies somewhere else. My fascination is games as a part of the wider culture. And this is where the indie scene shines. While the mainstream games are huge, impressive, and exciting amusement parks, created in a highly formalized, risk-averse way, smaller, independent games are where the experiments happen. A breeding ground of ideas, some of which could be seen as social commentary, poetry, moments of reflection, and even art.

I don't want to reopen the can of worms, which is the "Are games art?" discussion, so let's just make two notes on that topic. First, the critic who stated so firmly that games could never be art was a movie critic. This shows that transmedia parent-child issues could go both ways. Second, the argument and reactions to it kicked in the door and the idea that games *could* be art entered the public discourse.

This is, more or less, how we get where we are at the moment, as the video games industry. Which is where?

Are games still a growing medium? I think they are. We know how to make various types of games, and we have some ideas on how to make the games say things we want them to say. However, a lot of this knowledge is silent—with self-taught masters knowing *how* to achieve a desired effect, but having no idea *why* the way of doing things works. There is know-how, but I feel that we have problems with codifying and preserving said knowledge. It is usually passed, not always in a planned way, from a master to an apprentice if it is passed at all. So often when an employee leaves a project, their knowledge leaves with them.

On top of that, games are made using ever-changing software, and many tools and tricks are engine-specific and do not translate well to other projects, even within the same company. We are an innovative industry and indeed, we constantly innovate, something just because we failed to preserve the knowledge from previous projects. We still kick out too many open doors and lose too much knowledge in the process.

From the discussions with fellow game developers and my own experience, I would say that we need to establish theoretical foundations to discuss our goals and methods. To be able to consistently make art, we need more craft.

I have no doubt that we will get there. Movies also started as toys, plebeian recreation that couldn't even hold a candle to theater or opera. But over the decades, it took the medium to mature there were many growth spurts, where ground-breaking changes happened overnight. Some of the breakthroughs were technical, such as the leap from silent movies to voiced ones, or the dawn of black-and-white cinema, and the advent of color film. Others were conceptual when the way filmmakers thought about the production process or the artistic goals changed significantly. A good example would be the moment when Hollywood realized that Richard Burton and Elisabeth Taylor were much better in the intimate *Who's Afraid of Virginia Woolf* than in the bombastic and insanely expensive *Cleopatra*.

Video games also had their growth spurts. Technical breakthroughs were widely discussed elsewhere, so I will focus on those that had nothing to do with visual fidelity, and everything with finding new ways of telling intimate, emotional, true stories. Or at least, I'll mention games that I perceive as conceptual breakthroughs in the areas that interest me the most.

The idea that games could touch upon great ideas and stir deep emotions became clear in 1980 with *Missile Command*, a game about a doomed attempt to save cities from nuclear annihilation. It was an arcade shoot-em-up game, but the context was serious and well-aligned with the zeitgeist. But the idea that a game's sole purpose could be stirring emotions and providing reflection entered the public discourse in 2012 with the release of *Journey*, an aesthetically refined allegory of life disguised as a cozy adventure game. There were other similar attempts, such as the visual poem *The Graveyard* from 2008, but they were less commercially successful. Personally, the most emotional game I've played was 2021 *Before Your Eyes*, a game you played by blinking, where the very human physiology was used as a tool for immersion and reflection.

I also find interesting games that consciously try to explore and map the murky border between games and films. On one side of the spectrum, we have David Cage and his experiments with interactive movies, and various ways of combining the visual language of films with the UX and control schemes of games. In my opinion, the most interesting effects were reached in the flawed yet brilliant 2010s *Heavy Rain*. On the other side, we have Sam Barlow and his exploration of games where the very act of watching movies is gameplay. As for the moment of writing this book, he breaks new ground with every game, with the pinnacle being 2022s *Immortality*.

There is also the vibrant space of interactive fiction, where authors explore vulnerable topics that are close to home, tackling queerness, mental health, minority experiences, and history, and so creating a playable portrait of our times and a moving social commentary.

Mainstream games reach into the indie space for inspiration, and I'm glad they do so because the influx of radical and risky ideas gradually moves the goalposts for both developers and investors. Once upon a time, all a game had to provide was exciting gameplay, with a consistent narrative being an afterthought. Then, more and more mainstream games became story-driven or at least story-rich, when it became obvious that the same gameplay with a good story sells better. Now, the somewhat artificial barrier between gameplay and story dissolves (thank you *Half-Life 2* for proving that you can make a bestselling game with a captivating story and almost no cutscenes), and the idea that games can and perhaps should provide reflection and social commentary becomes widespread.

How far are we on this path from a toy to art? I am too close to say with any certainty. Is there already a game equivalent of *Citizen Kane*? I do not know and would love to hear your opinions.

One is sure. Games are here to stay. The industry grows steadily and even taking into account occasional hiccups and market collapses is already bigger than the movie industry. Thousands of titles are produced every year, and the impact of some of them will be visible in the years to come. From the business perspective, we are no longer in a small league; we've joined the big players.

You can see that in how video games are being presented in other media. Cultural magazines discuss new game releases with the same care they discuss new music albums, movies, or books. The old meme that video games cause violence still lives, but more often than not is being instantly debunked. Even movies stopped using games as a tool for showing that a character is immature and started presenting them as any other pastime. I think the turning point was when the 2013 Netflix political drama series *House of Cards* showed the protagonist, a presidential candidate, smoking weed and enjoying a game on his PlayStation. Video games have become cool. More importantly, they became normalized.

It is no wonder when you think about it. Players are getting older and older, and a generation that was born in a world where video games existed as mainstream entertainment has already reached adulthood. I was born in the late 1970s and for me, video games are, and probably always will be, the hot new thing. For my nephews, games are as obvious and natural as rain. This changes things.

There are still many challenges ahead. How to preserve and share knowledge? How to graduate the craft, change it from something that is taught and learned by hands-on experience into a discipline that could be consistently taught in a university environment? What stories to tell using the tools that we discovered? How to make art while still earning money for extremely expensive productions? There are many questions.

But it seems that all in all, video games are no longer perceived as toys. We are a serious industry that creates respected products that influence how people think and feel, that are critically analyzed and discussed, and that can and do—sometimes unwillingly—provide commentary on important social and political issues. There is little doubt that games can be art and the discussion moved on to when and in what way they are art. One of the most interesting YouTube videos about *Cyberpunk 2077* I've seen skipped the technical part completely and focused on a long analysis of the economic and ethical aspects of the game itself and the context in which it was made. If you ask me, sometime over the last ten years, video games found their place in the cultural landscape and can stand up to other, older, and more established media. Yes, they are specific. Yes, they require learning a specific language to be fully enjoyed. Yes, they are not for everyone. But so is ballet.

For the last half of the century, we fought a battle to be recognized as a serious medium. It seems that we have won.

Now, what?

2

WHY DO PEOPLE MAKE GAMES?

MARTA FIJAK

First, let's be frank. I'm a designer and this is a profession that sometimes requires a little bit of ego and hubris. Especially back in the old days when I was the only woman in a room full of boys, and the discussions were not based on arguments but on showmanship and rhetoric tricks*. There is also a lot of ego in deciding to write a book. It in itself is a statement that I think I know what I'm talking about. At least enough to write about it. Yet even with this amount of self-absorption and inflated ego, the question of why people make games is beyond me. At its heart, this is a question about the source of human creativity. Why are we like that? Why do we feel the need to create? Why, even when we were running after mammoths, we found the time to draw them on the walls of caves? A multitude of smarter-than-me people spent their whole lives trying to answer those questions. Still, there is no definite answer, but a multidimensional spaghetti of possibilities. So, I cannot dream about answering the question I posed. I'm sorry. Yet, what can I do is take you on a journey through time. We can examine why games (not only the electronic type) were created across the centuries. We can also look at why our fellow developers make them. We can even look at why I make games*.

> * It is much better now, as the notion that design is just coming up with ideas is slowly dying, and our profession "professionalizes." Also, those boys eventually became men. I also hope that I grew out of those old approaches.

> * Yup, definitely self-absorbed.

Maybe, among those different stories, you will find the answer to the question "why do you make games." Or maybe you already know it.

DOI: 10.1201/9781003325031-2

Let's start at the beginning of video game history. Ok, at least we think that this is the, as start. As archaeologists say, this thing is the oldest one, before we find an older one. We don't know if some scientists weren't playing some rudimentary games on oscilloscopes, laughing about what a silly thing they did with their equipment in the early 1950s*. There is also a question of what is a game, and if the game at hand is a true game. Yet, the definition of the game is a can of worms that I'm not going to open right now. Let's get back to the story, though.

* For sure, they did, as we are playful animals. I bet you dollars against donuts.

The year was 1958. World War II was still fresh in everybody's memory, and the Cold War was going strong. As you can imagine, after the Manhattan Project and with the constant threat of mutually assured destruction (MAD), physicists and laboratories have a moment of not the best PR.

This brings us to Brookhaven National Laboratory. Created a few years after the war, at first, its task was building a nuclear reactor. The public was not amused, to say the least. Rather more strongly distrustful and afraid. Mad scientists were doing mad things that would eventually lead to the death of us all, was the thinking at the time. So to ease the tensions, the laboratory had a yearly Visitor's Day. People would meet the scientists, see what they were doing, learn a little bit, and feel better about everything. For that special occasion, William Higinbotham*, one of the physicists employed there, had an idea to create something special. Something entertaining. A game!

* Yes, he also worked alongside Oppenheimer on the Manhattan Project.

With the help of technical specialist Robert V. Dvorak and using Donner Analog Computer Model 30, phosphor monochrome 5″ oscilloscope screen, and two controllers (consisting of a nob and a single button), the first game was born—*Tennis for Two**! As the name implies, it was a very rudimentary interpretation of tennis. You can imagine it as Pong but with a lot better

* At least, according to many, but of course, not everyone. That is the can-of-worms-type discussion on game definition that I will leave to ludologists.

physics. A lot.[1] The game was played by two players, where the button was responsible for hitting the ball and the knob for setting the angle at which it should be done. There was no fail state, and the game did not keep score, but at least a reset button was available. It was the biggest hit of the Visitor's Day that year, with queues to it that a modern Bethesda release would not be ashamed of. It fulfilled its purpose: people cheered and played it instead of being afraid. So yeah, the first video game was done as a PR stunt*.

Yet, *Tennis for Two* was never available commercially. We still had to wait for the lovely involvement of capital.

* It is a horrible simplification, I'm sorry. But it was a matter of bringing entertainment to an event whose goal was to ensure the public that nothing sinister was happening in the Lab.

To be precise, we needed to wait for Nolan Bushnell and Ted Dabney, who in 1971 released the first arcade game, *Computer Space*. Next year, their next mega-hit saw the light of the day— *Pong*. The world was never the same after that*. At the same time, the first genera- tion of consoles came into existence, with the release of Magnavox Odyssey in 1972. That's the one that was only

* There is also a whole story there, how *Pong* was "heavily inspired" by the *Table Tennis* game for Magnavox Odyssey. This "inspiration" ended with a lawsuit.

able to show a line and two dots, no sounds, controllers with a set of knobs (three of them), and a reset button. On top of that, there were semi-transparent screens in the box, which the player could stick to the TV to add more "graphic and excitement"*. It was the OG blue ocean time, as Magnavox did not fight for its market share. It created an entirely new market. Why was it created? It's hard to tell, but after going over in- terviews with its inventor Ralph Henry Baer, it seems

* The box was also filled with board game peripheries, such as money, dice, etc. What's even more fun, there were many games in the box on "cartridges." The fun part is that car- tridges did not contain any memory, they just reconfigured connections between console components.

that it came from the thought that it is a possible, creative need and that there may be a market for it. Those were the times when

TVs became a lot more affordable, and so more and more American families could get one. Bear, a military engineer, saw an opportunity there:

> *You know, I look at the set and say to myself, "What can I do with this?" There are forty million of them in the U.S., and another forty million of them elsewhere, and all I can watch here is stupid channels 5, 7, and 9 (...) and if I don't like what I see, all I can do is turn the damn thing off. (...) If I could just latch on to plugging something into a set for one percent of them, that's 400,000 sets. What the hell is wrong with that as a business objective?*[2]

From there the whole business party started. Atari 2600 entered the screen, followed by new versions of Magnavox and new competitors like ColecoVision. It was a gold rush. More games, more consoles, and more excitement on every corner. You probably know that this ended with a mountain of *E.T.* cartridges getting buried in New Mexico and the first, official video game crash (1983)*. The vibe at the time was that this was just a fad. A new children's toys craze, and as quickly it raised into popularity, it will be forgotten*. How wrong those people were, we know now. Yet, hindsight is always 20/20.

Instead of going in this direction*, let's move in the other direction. Leaving the world video behind, and sticking with games in general. It's time for the very old games! Like very very! Like 7000-year-old games.

* Thinking about this OG crash brings me some comfort, as this book was written during the "game industry market correction after COVID." We can also translate this name to mass layoffs and studio closure season.

* For my fellow Millennials—like Furby back in the day. Twenty years later, and I still want one, though.

* The next time we visit video games, it will be about shareware; so yes, there is a jump. No one promised a detailed history of video games, as there are amazing books about that topic. Not this one, though.

As we already stated, saying that something is "The Oldest Thing™" is a tricky business, so let's stay away from such radical claims.

Also, please take the years with a grain of salt, both due to inaccuracies that we have with dating artifacts, and also due to the fact I'm not an archaeologist*. Those are ballpark figures.

* But to my defense, I played a lot of *Tomb Raider* as a kid and watched all of the Indiana Jones movies.

We are playful creatures, some will even say that we are the Homo Ludens. Weirdly, this time around I do not mean Hideo Kojima*, but how it's defined by a Dutch philosopher—Johan Huizinga, in his impactful work—*Homo Ludens: A Study of the Play-Element in Culture* (1938)*. In there he claims that there is no culture without play, as play is a twin to culture, but one that was first. *"Play is older than culture, for culture, however inadequately defined, always presupposes human society, and animals have not waited for man to teach them their playing."*[3] The notion of fun and play was always with us, crossing the line between sacrum and profane, classes, and cultures. Play is a part of us that we cannot run away from. We are the Homo Ludens*.

* Because, at that time, this was the name of a studio he led.

* This is the book that the classic game definition comes from. You know, the one about clear rules, lack of impact on reality, win and fail, etc.

* It weirdly sounds like commercial for the Homo Ludens company, though.

Let's take a step further and move from play itself to games*. Objects created to provide a space for play. There is an idea that the first games were simple dice-based games, but this is just an assumption. The same as our assumption at the beginning of the chapter about scientists and oscilloscopes. We don't have enough evidence, only weirdly shaped bones found in early human camps. There are also concepts that clay tablets found in Ain Ghazal in Jordan, are elements of the first board game (dated at around ~5000 BC) but again, no concrete evidence.

* Still undefined, and I'm refusing to do it. The games discussed in this part are *games* games, though. Trust me on this one.

What we know is that board games existed for sure around ~3000 BC. We have three main competitors for the name of the oldest board game. Let's focus on two of them, both coming from Egypt—Senet and Mehen*. Both of them, are racing board games, similar in their gameplay to Ludo*. Why were those created? An impossible question to answer with full certainty. At this moment we are still not entirely sure what the rules even are. Yet, we can see how those games were a strong part of both sacred and profane. On one side, Senet slowly evolved to show the travels of the soul in the afterlife, and Mehen shares a name with one of the goddesses from ancient Egyptian beliefs (we don't know what was first). On the other side, we found Senet

* The third one is Game of Twenty Squares, also known as the Game of Ur, which comes from the city of Ur in Mesopotamia. It is also around 5000 years old and exists on the border of sacrum and profanum. Which of these three is the oldest one? Absolutely no idea.

* Also known as "Man, don't get angry" in some parts of Europe and "Chinese" in Poland. Why? As far as I was able to find out, it was because "exotic things were trendy at the beginning of the XX century." Yes, we still use this name. Yes, it is a problematic name.

boards carved in bricks, suggesting that workers played it during their breaks. There are also numerous paintings showing people playing it at all times and places—in houses, palaces, gardens, taverns, and even barber shops. Whether those games were originally created for fun or religious practices is hard to tell. David Emile Durkheim thought that games were created for religious purposes but flourished due to their social nature. Yet it could have been the other way around. We will never know what was first, the chicken, or the chicken nugget.

We know a little bit more about the reasons for the creation of chess, though. This game supposedly originates in the Indian peninsula. The oldest set that we found is dated to come from 760 A.D. This is not the same chess game as we play now. A prototype so to speak, that went through numerous iterations before we reached the stable release version that we know and play today. As far as the production timeline goes, around 700 years to polish the rule set is a perfect amount of time, in my opinion*. Yet, in this early version, we can more clearly see the purpose of the game. It was created as a training tool for army leaders. There are no women on the battlefield of

* The modern rules were created around 1475 in Spain. The final addition to the game was a woman! The Queen figure is said to be inspired by Queen Isabella I of Castile.

course, but all of the pawns were realistic depictions of elephant warriors, cavalry, infantry, etc. Those elephant warriors are also a reason why we think the game came from the Indian Peninsula.

Similar origins are assigned to Go. This one comes from ancient China. The first written evidence of its existence comes from the 4th century B.C. From there it traveled to Korea (around the 5th century AD) and Japan (7th century AD), where it found great success and a sea of admirers*. Who created it and why? Again, there is no consensus,

* Around 2004, it reached a small city in Poland, where it found me, also with great success.

but the legend says that Chinese Emperor Yao created it for his son, to teach him discipline, concentration, and balance. That's a legend though, and many scholars also find its origins in a training tool of army leaders. Of course, the line between sacrum and profane is thin, as some find its origins in a divination tool.

Those are of course not all only games that humans created and played, they are just some examples. We didn't even touch on the more notorious application of games—gambling*. Does not matter though, looking through these 7000 years of history, we still don't have a singular answer. Yet, a plethora of options emerge. Games were created because of religion, education, fun, social needs, PR, money, and market oppor-

* Remember the definition of a game problem? Huzinga, for example, does not define gambling games as part of play. They impact the "real world," which is a no-no for him. Yet, many of us design games with real-life impact, both monetary and as transformative/serious games.

tunity. Yet, looking at those early games, we can barely assume that technical flex was not the reason for their existence. Especially since the only way to improve the "rendering" of Senet or Go, or Chess, was probably hallucinogens, so not exactly a game development improvement. That changed dramatically though after the Atari era. To see that, let's travel to closer times—around 40 years ago. To the era of shareware games*.

* Shareware games were not the only ones taking part in the technological race. Let's be honest—it is still a motivation for creating some games today.

The year was somewhere between the 70s and 80s. Home computers just became a thing, with machines like Apple II, Atari 4000 and 8000, and the IBM personal computer. This opened the creation of software to a whole new group of people, both hobbyists and professionals. This time also posed new questions about the nature of software itself. In the early days, what was sold was the computers, not software. There was this idea that software should be free and accessible to everyone. Eventually, from this approach, a new business model was born: Shareware—free software. Users were encouraged to spread it as far and wide as they could. The only thing those programs had in terms of monetization was information in it that said "If you find this useful please pay me"*. This was a revolutionary, brave, and novel idea. This model has evolved over the years, with its ups and downs, stars and failures. That amazing period gave us both id Software and Epic, both originating from

* Today, we see a similar approach on itch.io. with the pay-what-you-want model, where some creators leave their ko-fi links in their software or how it is done by the world's most spread browser extension—AdBloc.

shareware space. What is interesting for us now is how some of those games came to be. The short answer is playing around the hardware limitations and showing what can be achieved.

Let's take, for example, *Commander Keen*—a side-scrolling platformer that was released on PCs in 1990 by id Software*. So how did this game come to be? It was the time of console domination. Nintendo was the top dog, both with their

* Yes, that id Software. It was their first game.

games and their consoles*. Frankly, all of the consoles were eons in front of the PC in terms of gaming. It sounds silly now, but you see, i.e., PCs couldn't do smooth scrolling backgrounds—that part that when you run to the side of

* Mario Bros was released in 1985 and took the world by storm. Nintendo Entertainment System (NES) was what every kid wanted to find under their Christmas tree. The Super Nintendo Entertainment System (SNES) was just around the corner.

the screen, there is more level that gets revealed in a nice, continuous way. That thing, due to hardware limitations, was a no-go for PC players. At least that was the assumption. Of course, as always in those situations, someone wanted to prove this assumption was wrong. This someone was John Carmack—the brilliant programmer who gave us *Wolfenstein*, *Doom*, and *Quake**. Before all of that though, he challenged himself with creating smooth scrolling backgrounds on PC and he succeeded. The path

* The fact that those games were created also had a lot to do with breaking the technical limitations.

from this first tech demo to *Commander Keen* was longer and more convoluted than this. It took almost a whole year and a team consisting of, now, legends of game development.[4] Funny enough, the first thing done with that tech was named *Dangerous Dave in Copyright Infringement**. Yet, *Commander Keen*, which eventually had seven installments in the series, started as a technical flex.

* It was, more or less, a PC clone of the first Mario level.

The next id Software mega-hit, *Wolfenstein 3D*, also came from the creation of a new shiny technology*. Yet id Software games were not the only ones that came out of technical pursuits.

* Ok, it was the third game made on this technology, preceded by *Hovertank 3D* and *Catacomb 3-D*.

Back in 1992, Nintendo released the first installment of *Mario Kart*. Apart from being a great game, and an awesome way to check the strength of friendships, it also used impressive feats of rendering trickery. This trickery is called Mode 7—a brilliant way of sprite manipulation to create a pseudo-3D space. This technology fascinated Andrew Edwardson (programming) and Shaun Gadalla (art). They painstakingly analyzed *Mario Kart,* to try to recreate this effect on the PC. From those efforts eventually *Wacky Wheels* was born—a Mario Kart-like game, where instead of carts, there were lawnmowers, and instead of Nintendo characters, we had animals.

Another example of that reason is *MicroMan* (1993). This game was created to show how action-packed and exciting games for Windows can be*. The issue with Windows games was, among other things, the lack of proper animation support. This was a challenge on which Brian Goble focused. The outcome of that was WAP—Windows Animation Package, and to show it a game was created— *MicroMan**. Yet, another title from that era, *Ken's Labyrinth*

* I know how it sounds now, but back then, there was Windows 3.0 with solitaire games, and DOS with all the cool things.

* It is not far from the first *Far Cry,* which started as X-Isle—a tech demo for the Crytek engine.

(1993) was created due to Ken Silverman's fascination with the technology of *Wolfenstein 3D.* First, he wanted to recreate it and then to make it better.

Technical flex was one of the reasons that games were made in that era (and still are), but going through the history of those times, there is also a second motivation popping up. Learning to code. If you've ever done that, you know what a monumental task this is. A whole new way of thinking. Wired vocabulary and syntax and constant errors that block you from compiling your code. You know the experience—you just learned what it means to compile, and now it does not work. Those beginnings required a lot of discipline and perseverance. Especially back in the day, when for something interesting to start happening with your program, a lot of lines had to be written. What always helps in those situations is having a project you want to finish, and what better project there is than creating a video game? This is the origin story of one of the most popular games for Macintosh—*Realmz.* Released in 1994, it took the Mac RPG-starved world by storm. Yet it started in an unlikely way. Tim Phillips just bought a new shiny Mac II and, on top of that, he was home stranded due to a knee injury. A perfect storm for creativity—what started as testing and playing with a new machine, ended as a full-fledged project, heavily inspired by the *Ultima* series. By the way, the first game that brought me any money was created for the same reason. When I got my first internship, they told me to learn Corona*. So, I had three months to find out about it as much as I could. This way *Edi: The Knight* (2014) was born—a set of nine minigames released as a single app on Android store*.

* A mobile game engine based on Lua.

* Fun fact—when I actually started that internship, they just switched to an early version of Unity, and all of that Corona learning was useless. Ok, not true. I released, on my own, two more games using it.

As time progressed, we matured as a medium. A lot of things came with, but also, the accessibility of development itself. Now you can make a game without writing a single line of code. Engines available to the masses, allow hobbyists to do things that were reserved only for top programming brains. Now I can have a full TPP setup, with procedural animations and animation states, content editor, physics, collisions, etc. in two days of work.[5] There are also courses, YouTube videos, university degrees, books, and even podcasts about game-making. Learning to do it was never as easy as it is now. All of this brought a whole new group of people to making games, with a whole new set of motivations to do it.

For example, serious games—games with a bigger purpose than entertainment itself*. A puzzle video game *Fold It* was released in 2008. It has a thriving community to this day that logs in every day to solve spatial problems, by bending big structures. This community has been mentioned in many scientific papers as contributors. Some of them were published in such prestigious magazines like Nature*. Why? Because those mega-structures folded in the game are models of real-life proteins. The trick

* Still, games as only entertainment are very valid. J. Shell now proposes the term "transformative games" to combat the problem with this term.

* For non-biological-sciences people—Nature is THE magazine you want to publish in.

with proteins is that they have few levels of construction. One thing is from what amino acids they are constructed, but another thing is what is their three-dimensional construction. Usually, they are not just long chains of connected parts. They create an interactive web of elements that bend and curve around each other. To predict how they will bend is a non-trivial task. Yet we know the rules that this folding process follows. So why not translate those rules for a scoring system and give the players a space to min-max it? This is exactly what *Fold It* is. It harvests our natural tendency to solve puzzles and our spatial imagination, to discover this higher order of proteins. Then, those best player generated solutions are analyzed by scientists and eventually push our global understanding of the world around us. This is not a happy accident of design. This is the way the game was created by the University of Washington, Center for Game Science, and the UW Department of Biochemistry.

Another such game is the *Sea Hero Quest*. Why did this game come to be? Lack of good data for early Alzheimer's screening. One of the early symptoms of Alzheimer's is a decline in navigation skills. Yet, it's hard to create a proper baseline for it, as it requires tracking our control group participants in space. As you can imagine, it's problematic to make large case studies this way. This is where the game is an answer. *Sea Hero Quest* is exactly that—a cut VR game about navigation that allowed the collection of data from 4.3 million players.[6]

Those are just two examples of serious games, but there are a lot more of thrm. Why were they created? Because people wanted to solve a real-life problem with a game. Some of them are used in physical therapy (*Rapids Recovery*), others teach people about menstruation (*Go Nisha Go*), and there are even games out there that teach people how to perform real-life surgeries (*Pulse!*)*.

* Even if you beat this game, please do not operate on your friends without a proper license.

With this accessibility of tools and knowledge, another motivation also entered the scene with more power than ever—self-expression. Suddenly a lot more people could make games in a shorter time. So people started to share things important to them in the form of games. It was not a new phenomenon, as the first known game touching LGBTQ+ topics was released in 1989*. Yet, since 2010, there has been an explosion of games that told strong personal stories, such as: *Depression Quest* (2013), a game depicting the everyday struggle of people with this illness; *That Dragon Cancer* (2016), an autobiographical game about being with a young kid who is dying of cancer; or *Dys4ia* (2014), a game about struggles with body dysmorphia and transitioning.

*It was *Caper in the Castro*. It is a great talking point when someone is telling you that new games are bad due to inclusion. Nah, my dude, inclusion was always there, in one form or another.

Those things that people want to express are not always autobiographical; sometimes people want to put the spotlight on current events by making games. From this space, we have games like *Bury Me, My Love* (2019), following Syrian refugees on their journey to Europe, or *Terra Nil* (2023), which allows the player to rejuvenate barren wastelands to lush green spaces. Those are just examples, but with the democratization of tools, games become a full-flagged way of expression—thanks to Unity, Game Maker, etc., creators can focus more on what they want to say and less on how to render anything to the screen*. This way, another reason emerged very strongly, as processing difficult topics through art and creation is a motivation as old as time.

*I know it sounds funny now, but when I started, free engines were in their infancy. The first challenge I had to overcome was to learn how to draw stuff on the screen before I could start thinking about anything else.

We are in the indie space though, and in a particular part of it. Those games are created to reach an audience, but the profit motive is not the main reason for their existence. I'm not native; I know that the profit undertone is present in all commercial releases, but many games are created not only for this. There are other motives. Bringing joy to players, telling a certain story, exploring a new fresh gameplay, etc. Yet, there are games whose sole reason to exist is to multiply the money of the stakeholders. I'm writing this while a great game industry correction is happening. After the COVID-19 boom and before this stock market boom*, the trend is set the other way. More than 6000 developers lost their jobs, and projects were canceled left and right. Some of those projects though were or are being created, just because an unused IP is lying around. Of course, the developers to this day are trying to make something out of it*, but the sole reason for the creation of some games is money. Recognizable intellectual property for a while seemed to be a protection for investment, and a promise of big returns. If something has Lord of the Rings attached to it, it will sell for sure, so let's make another game in that universe. Especially, since people work in this business out of passion, they can have a budget way too small, and overtime is not paid at all. This will make the final profit so much sweeter and bigger. In those conditions, *The Lord of the Rings: Gollum* was born. The game currently has 4% on OpenCritic* and sold less than 35,000 copies.[7] Before that fiasco though, I can not tell you* how many meetings I took, where investors slapping an IP onto an existing prototype was the first. Did the IP make sense? Not always, but having an IP was seen as better and more sure than a fresh concept. This pushed the development of those projects into a Frankenstein monster construction site. On one side, there were developers who just want to make a good game; on another side, IP holders with their vision of the IP; and on the third side, investors with their understanding of the gaming market. Due to the game's boom, many of those investors were not familiar at all with games yet; they have the money, so they have the power. This created

* Before 2022, the Polish stock market was a gaming El Dorado. It was enough to have "game" in the company name, and the investors would explode with cash.

* Usually.

* To put this in perspective, *Forspoken*, which was not well-received, has 30%, and *Ghostwire: Tokyo*, which was met with mixed reception, has 67%.

* NDA

situations when the investor's nephews played a game and due to their opinion, a whole direction of development got changed.

The second tactic was cloning an already existing successful game, just to grab a little bit of the sweet money pie. Extraction shooter is a thing? Let's make one. Multiplayer minigames with the theme of falling are a thing. Let's make one of those! A narrative story of the plague sold many copies. Hell yeah, let's jump on that train. This gold rush also created a much bigger demand for developers, so this, paired with inflation and other things, ballooned the development cost. A perfect setup for a bursting bubble, but this is not an essay about that.

Don't get me wrong, games need to make money*. So we can make more games, yet it

* At least, in the current system.

seems that if the only reason for the game to exist is that, no one is going to have a good time.

A cynical example of this profit motive is the Playway market analysis approach.[8] The idea is simple. Create as many game trailers as you can—different simulator games to make it easy. Examples include Plumber Simulator, Carpenter Simulator, Priest Simulator, Rat Simulator, etc. To be clear, none of those games is in production, just the trailers. Put the trailers on steam. Observe the wishlists. Who gets enough wishlists, gets made. As simple as that. Currently steam is fighting with this tactic by changing the requirements for the steam page content. Yet, this tactic is very profitable for Playway*. The owner of the company, Krzysztof Kostowski, compares this model to Kickstarter.[9] I do not agree, at least on principle, with this take. Kickstarter games are there because someone wants to create them, not to check if they will sell*.

* Playway is in the top 3 of gamedev companies traded on the Warsaw stock exchange.

* I know that this is not always the case, especially in recent years. Please do not burst my bubble of hope, though.

This cynical money-making mentality is a segway to why developers make games. I do not have a proper study for this. I just walked around and asked the question

"Why do you make games?" This way I collected around 250 answers. Some of them are from hobbyists, some are from indies, and others are from seasoned triple-A developers. After many conferences, coffees, dinners, and DMs, I sat down with all of the data. The answers fell more or less into four categories: "Childhood exposition," "Sending the rocket to Mars mentality," "Self-expression," and "I'm stuck." We already covered the self-expression part, and as it is crucial among the indies, it also pops up from time to time among AAA people, which are mostly artists and designers. So let's move to the other three categories, starting from the first one.

Childhood exposition is the most obvious one. We even have a saying in Poland just about that: "What an eggshell absorbs when young, this is how it smells when old."* As far as I understand, "what youth is used to, age remembers" is the English equivalent of that. So, this

* Don't ask me why, I'm just exposing you to the beauty of my language.

comes up in answers many times that there is something magical in this moment when you press a button/screen and suddenly something changes. Suddenly, we are not passively absorbing the fun on the screen; we are part of it. More so, in the very center of it! It does not matter the generation. It's as magical with the first *Super Mario Bros* as it is with *Minecraft* and *Roblox*. Kids can not get enough, and some of them grow up to make those experiences for the next generations. It is as simple and pure as that.

"Sending the rocket to Mars mentality" comes more from engineers (not only though) and more from AAA people. It touches on this magical aspect of games that they are an outcome of art and engineering, and you will never know what part of the project will catch fire at any given moment. There is a challenge in that, a puzzle to be solved, over and over again. Some people are drawn to that. Not only on a purely technical level but also in terms of a new storytelling medium. How can I tell what I want using these tools? How can I push this medium further? What has not been done in games yet? A competition in creativity and problem-solving, and at the same time a marathon in craftsmanship.

The final group, "I'm stuck," seems to me to be connected to those money-making incentives*. People in gamedev get burned out; it's a tale as old as this medium. They join the industry full of passion and dreams. Then, they fall into a developer meat grinder. Projects

> * Not only though. In general, it seems connected with bad business management. Yet, those answers mostly came from people stuck in those "quick money grab" projects. On a side note, some of those "quick" grabs are seven years in the making.

that are lost in the lack of direction and vision forest for years. Crunch culture makes work-life balance a joke. A quick cash-grab project where craftsmanship has to be sacrificed for profit. All of the usual. When you ask those people why they make games, there is sometimes sadness in their eyes, for the passion they lost. Sometimes it's not that, sometimes they are just empty. The answer I got usually was something along the lines of "It's the only thing I know how to do to make money," or "I'm stuck with the skills I have. Forever in this hell hole of an industry." I know this state does not have to be permanent. Sometimes they change the company or take a long leave and the spark for game-making is back. Sometimes though, they stay like this, in misery, in constant performative passion for games mode, as this is expected of them. Dying on the inside every day a little bit more, while cheering for another project direction change*. Then, if they can, they quit games altogether. We all know those stories.

> * Not pretending may damage their livelihood.

As we come from that depressive perspective, it's time for me to answer the question posed in this essay—Why do I even make games? Like in the rest of this essay, there is no one concrete answer to that question, but rather a multidimensional spaghetti that fluctuates through time. The need arose in the 90s. I saw an Amiga at my uncle's flat. I pressed a button and a frog[10] on the screen moved. I was ecstatic. It seemed like magic. My uncle was huge into computers and I mostly lived with him as a child, so I had access to his hardware. I fell in love with *SuperFrog*, *SocerKid*, *North and South**, and

> * I had absolutely no idea how to play that one, but it seemed to be many games in one, and I always had my fingers crossed for the train level.

The Last Samurai. Then, he got his first PC, the technological leap scrambled my tiny child brain. *Duke Nukem 3D* was a whole world I was able to explore and interact with*! My fate was sealed! Ok, that's not exactly true, as I thought that making games was as feasible of an idea as being an astronaut*. Still, though, this dream of making those amazing things became a part of me. My uncle coded projects for his degree—he used Borderland Delphi, an IDE that had an integrated graphical interface-creating tool. I was 8, so coding was not an option*, but I was able to create whole "spaceship command centers" from those UI elements, and then click on them for hours, pretending that buttons did something.

> * A few years later, I realized that maybe it was not the best place for a kid, as I finally understood why I was giving money to those ladies, and what was that movie that played in the cinema on the first level. It was porn.

> * I was a girl in the middle of Poland, and the only Polish game I knew about was *The Prince and the Coward.*

> * Now, I teach kids this young the basics of coding. It was a different time, though.

This childhood sense of wonder stayed with me for years. I played everything I could find and learned as much as I could about games. The game maker also became a thing, so I started to make silly little things. I thought it was childish though, so it was time to decide about my future. Games were not an option for me, so I went to pursue a degree in Experimental Biology and Genetics. There were a few shenanigans in those years, but the "too-long, didn't read" version is that I pursued a second degree in Computer Science to supplement my work as a biologist. This allowed me to do a computer science internship. So I dressed all pretty, made a video of all my university projects, and went to Techland. The interview went great, until the last part, when they asked me how much money I would like to make during the internship. I got so bloody excited that I said "It's games! I don't need money!"* I got the internship. It was everything I ever wanted. I worked on games eight hours a

> * I'm ashamed of that answer. Labor is labor and it should be paid, but I was very young and very excited. I also was able to support myself through other means during the internship.

day, next to people with the same passion and so much knowledge. I did not stay with them after the internship—they

> * After that, I spent two weeks as a full-blown burrito of sadness.

told me they wanted me, but there is no budget*. Yet, it refueled my dream. After watching Indie Game: The Movie, I realized this path was an option. I thought I would make games at night, and by day I would be a proper biologist.

I released some games, with good reception, but no big financial success. The issue was that my biology path was not making any money. Nice and shiny letters in front of my name, but no money. So after some more shenanigans*, I got my first proper (paid!) job in gamedev.

> * I wanted to win a tablet in a game design contest; I did not get the tablet, but I got a job.

In a F2P company, as a data analyst. This is the first time I had to confront the question "Why do I make games" after so many years. Why? My job was pinpointing how we could make more money out of our players. I was good at it, but after the first month, I cried every day I came back home. This was not what I hoped for, it was not creating joy for people, it was squeezing them dry. I stayed though. I fought to be switched to design. It made it slightly better. Yet still, thinking about games as hobbies and pushing people into conversion* rubbed me the wrong way. The work was good though, I

> * i.e. making a purchase in a F2P game.

was paid well for that moment in my career, the job had a great work-life balance, the team was awesome, etc.

The itch of this broken dream stayed with me. This is not why I wanted to make games. Eventually, an opportunity arose: an option to start working at the studio of my dreams*. Yes, I needed to move 300 km. Yes, the salary was lower, and yes, the work-life balance would

> * This War of Mine made me see games in an entirely different light—I loved it as a concept.

change dramatically. I took the jump. I was older and more mature, but the old passion came back. What's more, outside of making something amazing for the players, I found a new layer to it—games could tell important things, not just entertainment, but a medium of expression! I was hooked again and hooked so strongly that the idea of work-life balance seemed a joke to me. Then, after 2.5 years, *Frostpunk* was released. A new, darker motivation to make games appeared, which is outside validation.

This outside validation combined with work being the most important part of my life* brought me to the darkest time in my career. A difficult project, burnout, emotional

> * My wife is a saint because she did not leave me back then.

breakdown, health decline. The whole shebang. After two years of that, I didn't know if I wanted to make games. Yet, that was my career, what else I was going to do? I wanted to quit many times, yet, from that whole sorry show a new motivation came. I was a lead back then. I couldn't leave, as I didn't want to leave my team. My goal was to protect them and give them space to make games. I found glimpses of hope in that. Following that, I started to teach more, not bringing people joy by making games, but by teaching them to make games. This gave me strength.

Eventually, I quit and joined a different company. I was afraid that the reason to make games was gone. Only this fragile ego's need for outside validation was left. That was not true. It took a set of long conversations with myself, my wife, and a therapist, but eventually, I got rid of these bollocks. In this space, the old motivation reappeared, the childlike wonder, but more mature now, with this layer of pushing the medium as far as I can. It's a new, exciting way for me to communicate with people and bring them joy. I'm good with this motivation. I hope it will stay.

So, why do you make games?

Notes

1 You can also just watch a gameplay video here: https://www.youtube.com/watch?v=6PG2mdU_i8k&ab_channel=TheDotEaters
2 https://www.gamedeveloper.com/business/the-right-to-baer-games—an-interview-with-ralph-baer-the-father-of-video-games
3 Huizinga 1955, p. 1.
4 Tom Hall, John Carmack, John Romero, Adrian Carmack, Robert Prince.

5 https://x.com/YerisTR/status/1680593826153480192?s=20

6 https://www.alzheimersresearchuk.org/research/for-researchers/resources-and-information/sea-hero-quest/

7 https://playtracker.net/insight/game/85831?utm_source=SteamDB

8 https://www.wired.com/story/playway-polish-simulator-game-company/

9 https://gameworldobserver.com/2021/09/03/how-publisher-playway-strives-by-promoting-dozens-of-steam-games-that-might-never-come-out

10 *SuperFrog*, to be exact. A platformer, released in 1993.

3

THE MYTH OF THE UNIVERSAL AUDIENCE

ARTUR GANSZYNIEC

This is a story from the outskirts. Many such stories are happening all around the world, but I will focus on the one I witnessed firsthand.

To set the context, let's say you come from an East-European country, with a population roughly the same as the population of the State of California. The year is 2010 and you realize that making games has become easier than ever before. Together with your three friends, you can make a viable, high-quality product in half a year, maybe nine months, ship it, and wait for the revenue to come in. Unfortunately, when you look at the numbers, you can also see that your local market is too shallow to sustain your production. If you relied only on the games sold in your country, you would never break even.

Luckily for you, with a single click, you can ship the game worldwide. You just have to make it in English. This is not a big problem, as the game is text-light, and you've all learned English anyway. And if the game is in English, it would be able to sell on almost all markets. Who doesn't speak English nowadays, especially if they are gamers? In the future, if your game is successful, you can think of making localized versions and selling even more. But for now, with the limited budget you have, you create the game just in English, publish it worldwide, and the world is your oyster.

The game hits the market and soon you start receiving reviews, feedback, and emails from all over the world—from the USA, Brazil, Germany, Australia, and maybe even China. You've made a relatively successful, mass-culture product, targeted at everyone, and you can bask in the glory of a creator, who transcended the borders of your

DOI: 10.1201/9781003325031-3

home country. Tens of thousands of players have found a reflection of their experiences in your game, and if you work on making the game even more universal, that number could reach hundreds of thousands, maybe even millions of people. You just have to tap into the universal, human experience.

At least that's what I thought at that time. We talked about it a lot, and it seemed pretty straightforward—if you see something of yourself in the game, you will have a better time with it, and you will probably play it more and talk about it more. All we needed to do was to open the game to points of view and experiences that weren't ours and make the game more inclusive and more universal. It seemed to me that the ideal, universally universal game, appealing to every player regardless of their background and country of origin, existed and was within our reach.

If I looked closer at the messages and feedback we got, I might have noticed that the actual reception of particular elements of the game differed slightly, depending on where the player was from. But, I didn't. When in doubt, it was natural to default to what the American players said, as the American market accounted for about half of the sales. Besides, we all grew up on movies made in Hollywood and video games made in the USA. Following this train of thought, if something was understandable in America, it was as good as universal.

This approach worked for a few years until it turned out that the Chinese market became as big and important as the American. Suddenly, it became very important to learn and cater to the small peculiarities of the Chinese audience. It would be better if there were no skulls in the game, it would be better to remember that the number 4 is considered bad luck in China. I'm not talking here about political censorship, as our games were not legally available in China, I'm talking about the preferences of the players, stemming from the culture they grew up in. There were more such peculiarities in the other markets as well (e.g. as a rule, Americans have more problems with sex than violence, while Europeans have more problems with violence than sex), but they just weren't so important. By this, I mean that the peculiarities observed in markets were too small to influence sales in any significant way.

So what is the recipe for a universally appealing game? First, include as many points of view and experiences as you can, while keeping the whole game consistent, and then remove everything that could offend players from any of the countries you target the game to. So, you just have to cut nipples for Americans, blood for Germans, and skulls for Chinese—the list would be quite long, especially if we take into account what is legally mandatory in each country (no swastikas in Germany), what the audience of this particular genre demands (no pentagrams in Hidden Object Puzzle Adventures, because of the Texan housewives), or what the most vocal players demand (should we listen to the "not enough inclusivity" group, or the "to much wokeness" group, or just cut everything that could offend any of them?). But theoretically, if we managed to cut any potentially offensive content, what remains would be universally understandable and appealing, wouldn't it?

It seems that it's not always the case, as the following examples show.

Frostpunk is a city-building survival game developed by 11-bit studios and released in 2018. It tells a story of alternative Victorian times when a new ice age came and drove life on Earth to the brink of extinction. You take care of the Last City, managing both resources and human tempers. One of the tools at your disposal is deciding the laws that govern your community. Usually, the harsher the conditions, the harsher laws seem to be optimal for your city's survival. When the game ends, it shows you a time-lapse of your settlement's development, showing its gradual shift toward a totalitarian nightmare. The time-lapse ends with the question "The city survived. But was it worth it?" If we survived as a ruthless tyranny, are we still who we were before? This is a perfectly understandable question. Or so the creators thought until they started receiving messages from the Chinese players, who were sure there was some bug or mistranslation in the game's final moments. Because the fact that the city survived automatically means that it was worth it, doesn't it? The problem of the survival of society versus personal survival and freedom is framed so differently in Western culture versus how it is understood in China that the very moral of the game proved untranslatable between the two cultures. A question that seemed so understandable that almost banal for one group of players made literally no sense for another group. I thought about the problem a lot and had the chance to talk with *Frostpunk's* creators and ask for their opinions, and still, I'm not sure how, or if, you could "fix" the issue and make the ending equally understandable and impactful in both Europe/USA and China. We could, of course, just drop the issue, show the time-lapse, and ask no hard questions, but the artistic and emotional value of the game would surely suffer.

Unpacking is a cozy, slow story/puzzle game where you observe someone's life by unpacking their things after moving into new apartments. It was one of my games of 2021, and I think it is a masterclass in environmental storytelling. I had *opinions* about the protagonist's life choices without ever seeing her or her friends in the game. I celebrated her successes and was saddened by her setbacks, which I deduced while taking her things out of cardboard boxes, and placing them in the appropriate rooms. There was just one moment when I was lost and a bit frustrated. There was this bottle of washing detergent that wouldn't fit anywhere in the bathroom. Not on the floor, not in the closet, not under the sink, not behind the toilet, not on the washing machine, not under the shower. I had to find a walkthrough on the Internet and learn that the bottle should be placed in the kitchen. But why? The answer was simple—it was a bottle of orange juice, not washing detergents. But I've never shopped in an American grocery store, and in Europe orange juice usually comes in cardboard boxes or standard plastic bottles. The culture I grew up in made me blind to the solution that was obvious, even transparent, for any American. It was not a big issue, and I'm bringing it only to illustrate a little moment that spoiled the game's universality.

The Witcher 3 is an action RPG game, loved by players and critics alike. It tells the story of a mutant monster hunter looking for his adopted daughter in a world torn by war and famine. The game uses dark fantasy as the scene to show and comment on very current issues, and the consensus is that it does the job well. There is just one topic that stirred controversy on many websites and social networks—the issue of racism. The game is set in a fictional, pseudo-medieval setting, and all the characters are white. For understandable reasons, this was commented upon by people of color, who didn't find themselves and their experiences reflected in the games. But how can you say that the game is racist?—retorted East-European players—as one of the main themes of the whole series is the prejudice against elves and other non-humans, and the daily experiences of the main character who is persecuted for his ancestry? The two vocal groups clashed, which resulted in several interesting articles and hundreds of very unpleasant flames. The problem was, in my opinion, that both groups—within their experiences—were right. The game was indeed created by Polish creators, based on a series of books by a Polish author, which originally commented on the Polish reality of the late 1990s. And Poland, due to its complicated history, is a country where over 90% of the population is ethnically Polish, and almost everyone is white. In the country's history, there was, and still is, a lot of prejudice and xenophobia, but it was connected not with the color of the skin, but with the language one used, nationality, economic status, or ancestry. When building the critique of racism and xenophobia into their game, *The Witcher 3*'s creators built on their experiences—in a way that was clearly understandable to European players and totally irrelevant to the Americans. This is, again, a problem without a clear and easy solution. Would adding people of color to the game be anything but tokenism, when the writers have no experience whatsoever with the realities of racial interactions in today's America? At the same time, the writers' own experiences with prejudice and xenophobia turned out to be irrelevant and illegible to an important section of the players.

When I considered those examples, my hope that there could be a universal game targeted at the universal audience started to unravel. It hit me that even the universal audience I believed in was a myth.

Frankly speaking, each time, when we tweaked our games to better fit the "universal audience," we tweaked it to better fit the American market because the American market drove most of the sales.

As a designer and writer, this is a tough place to find myself in—to create games in a language that is not my own, for a culture that's not mine, and for the players from a country I've visited three times in my life and have never lived in.

Because my goal is still, to make games that will speak to as many players as possible. There are at least two reasons for that. First, the money. Making games is expensive, and you need to resonate with as many players as possible to reach your target numbers and make ends meet. Second, and personally more important to me, I love it when people play my games, and each time, when I see that I find a way to entertain (or move) someone whose life is very different from mine, I feel immense joy and satisfaction.

Yet, it is hard. When designing and writing, I cannot rely solely on my daily experiences, and I have to look critically at things that are transparent to me. Returning to the issue of race—I cannot write characters as I see them every day on the streets, because in the town I live in, almost everyone is white. If I uncritically copied and pasted what I saw into a game, I would alienate many players that I was interested in reaching—although I would be telling a story that would be true. So first, I have to adapt what I see, to the culture that I'm writing for. Distance the game from my own experiences and push it closer to the experiences of the potential players.

So how do I educate myself about the culture I write for? I spend time on the English-speaking Internet, watch American movies, play American games, read American books, and watch American news. But there is a problem—most of my sources are pop culture. Pop culture is not reality, it is reality chewed and spewed by others, reality tinted by the creators' worldviews, and the reality experienced second-hand. What's worse, in some cases, my pop culture sources are dated and show the world in a way that is no longer relevant, and maybe even offensive. Also, I do not always have the knowledge to spot that. To me, working in such a way feels like trying to make small intricate sculptures while wearing thick winter mittens. It is possible, but not easy.

There is one other can of worms that I choose not to open in this chapter—the issue of cultural appropriation, and the question of whether and when you can create based not on your own experiences, but trying to show things from the point of view of someone not belonging to your own culture. This is a huge topic, and I don't feel equipped to tackle it at the moment.

But is this writing for the dominant (American, Chinese, pick your type) marker really a necessity? The aforementioned *The Witcher 3* was a huge success, and one of the things universally praised was its Slavic aesthetics. So, maybe I'm overreacting, and players worldwide are waiting for non-American motifs and stories written from the local point of view? That might be true, at least when we're talking about the aesthetics, decorations, and visuals. But if we risk a deeper dive, we may soon crash against the wall of differing life experiences and cultural associations—as *The Witcher 3* race debacle clearly showed.

I write this and find myself thinking—and what about games made in Japan? They are clearly made for the Japanese market, and yet they are successful worldwide, and they surely do not care if their appeal is universal. Most of them are either very focused on Japanese culture or are picking and mixing Western themes and motifs as they see fit. I still remember the wonderful turmoil in my head that was caused by the *Eternal Sonata*, which was a turn-based role-playing game, where I battled animated plants, and it all was a dream of the most Polish of composers, Fryderyk Chopin. Or let's take the blue-skinned militarist foreigners in *Ghost Trick: The Phantom Detective*—who were they? Was the game made with the universal audience in mind? Clearly not. And yet, it was successful, as were many other Japanese games. When I think about it, I see three factors that can explain the situation. Most of the games that made it worldwide had great gameplay that spoke for itself. At the same time, Japanese pop culture is quite popular in the West—sometimes to the point of fetishization—so the players had a better base understanding of the developers' culture compared to games made in Estonia or Iran. Finally, the Japanese market is big enough for most of the games to reach the break-even point locally. Their creators didn't pander to the "universal" market because they didn't have to. I love many Japanese games, yet I still feel unease each time a good guy wears clothes that are nothing but a slightly repainted Nazi uniform.

When I started working in the game dev industry, I thought that there was one universal audience that I could reach, making my game equally accessible in all countries around the world. With time, my perspective shifted. The longer I make games, the more I see that this "universal" audience was the audience from the market that sold the most copies of the game—which usually meant that I had to tailor the game to the needs and tastes of the American players.

At first, I thought that the way to make this and still keep some local insights intact was to add as many inclusive and widely understandable elements and then remove all content that could be offensive or unclear in the most important markets.

In reality, this usually means tailoring the game either to the American or the Chinese market. And the *Frostpunk* ending is just one example of how an element clearly understandable in one of the cultures is indecipherable in the other. The cross-cultural misunderstanding could be small, like the orange juice bottle in *Unpacking*, or quite crucial, like *The Witcher 3* race debacle. The solution—for creators from smaller countries—is to learn to create games for an America or from the American-adjacent point of view. Only big markets, like Japan, can afford to create games for the local sensibilities and rely on the foreign players' knowledge of local pop culture while selling the game abroad. For the rest, perhaps the best they can count on is using local aesthetics as the market edge, making games that *look* different but tell stories easily understandable in the USA.

Wait a minute, there must be games that tell stories set in a particular culture, focused on local problems, which have succeeded worldwide. I can't think of many examples.

There was *Kingdom Come: Deliverance*, a story-driven open-world RPG set in medieval Bohemia, very historically accurate and Czech to the core. It was critically acclaimed and sold very well.

There was *1979 Revolution: Black Friday*, an adventure interactive drama video game set in Iran and telling about the Iranian Revolution in an attempt to overthrow the Shah. It gained critical acclaim but was not a commercial success.

There is *Disco Elysium*, the famous Estonian detective role-playing game with a distinctive oil painting art style. It is set in a fictional country in a fictional world, but—at least for East-Europeans—its main theme of post-Soviet nostalgia is clearly visible and instantly understandable. It's hard for me to say if the themes resonate at all with the Western audience and if the same game set in real post-Soviet Estonia would gain any traction.

Maybe there are other examples, but at the time, none came to my mind.

Sometimes, when I think about it all, I feel like a craftsman living in the distant reaches of the empire, working on products that he hopes will sell in distant Rome, which he knows only from the stories he heard from travelers and merchants.

There's this Hollywood saying that if a story is personal enough it becomes universal, and it seems to work for movies. I hope that, sooner or later, it will also apply to games.

Because, frankly, I'd love to see more games that would try to reach the mythical universal audience not by mimicking America or China and their (pop) culture, but by a detailed, honest, and personal focus on the culture and experiences of one of the small countries their developers come from. I would love to play more stories from the outskirts.

4

TRAPS OF REALISM

ARTUR GANSZYNIEC

Many years ago, I was working on *The Witcher*, the first video game in the franchise. When we were nearing the end of the production, we invited Andrzej Sapkowski, the acclaimed Polish fantasy author, and creator of Geralt of Rivia—our protagonist—and the world our game was set in. We were very anxious about how he would react and how he would comment on the game because he was known for his sardonic wit that spared nothing and no one. Yet, it went down in a very civilized way. He watched a hands-off presentation of the game and said: "It looks nice. Much better than I thought it would." He commented on nothing else.

As disappointed (and relieved at the same time) as I was that he said nothing about the dialogues or the story, for which my team was responsible, I realized that this is how most people perceive games—as a visual medium. So, the first criterion people use to judge the quality of a game is its looks. And for the standards of the year 2007, *The Witcher* looked nice enough.

When I am writing this chapter, in 2023, it's hard for me to look at *The Witcher* and not cringe a little. Geralt looks so angular and his facial animations are almost non-existent. Side characters all look almost the same and can be recognized only by their displayed names. The closer the camera is to the objects in the game, the easier it is to notice the low quality of the textures. And let's not even talk about the fact that to jump over a fence, our mighty monster slayer needed an in-engine cutscene.

But when the game came out, it looked nicer than expected. It definitely wasn't on the cutting edge of rendering technology, but how it looked was good enough. Now, it's not.

Video games are, for better or worse, a visual medium and the visual side has been the driving force of technological progress in the

 DOI: 10.1201/9781003325031-4

games industry. With better hardware, better rendering techniques, higher quality models, textures, and animations, the progress curve is getting steeper every year. The assumed goal of this arms race is the perfect visual fidelity; games that would look like "reality."

The visual aspect of a game is commented on in most reviews, sometimes with more scrutiny than the gameplay, while the story or the moral of the game is just a footnote. How many frames per second (FPS)? Is the ray tracing used? Are animations clipping? How realistic is the water simulation? What elements of the environment are destructible? Late titles on any generation of consoles are being praised for squeezing everything there was to squeeze from the setup. At first, it's all about the look.

I want to be clear, I'm not saying that look is not important. You shouldn't judge a book by its cover, but you may judge a game by its screenshots. The topic that I want to discuss is the pressure on "realistic" graphics that exists in our industry. And when we say "realism," we usually mean "visual fidelity." We want things in games to look exactly as they look in real life.

From a creator's perspective, this push toward visual realism has interesting consequences.

Before we dive in, I feel obliged to write a quick disclaimer about the terminology. When we look at the way the word "realism" is used in the arts, we see that it is a movement focused on representing subject matter truthfully, and avoiding speculative and supernatural elements. In this meaning, almost no game is "realistic." The term we should be using is "naturalism," which is the idea of depicting subject matter—objects of art—with the least possible amount of distortion and highest visual fidelity. But since no gamer has ever said that a game doesn't look "naturalistic" enough, I also will stick with the common usage.

Besides, it is one of those "a rose by any other name ..." problems. No matter what we call it, the pressure on the visual fidelity of games is one of the forces shaping our industry today.

It is the look that distinguishes Little Ligue from the Big Boys. We look at a screenshot or a gameplay capture and we instantly know whether we look at an AAA game or at an indie production. Or, at least, we create an opinion on that matter. This mechanism of first impressions is very simple: high visual fidelity, fluid animations, and a rich world mean the real, mainstream digital entertainment, while low-poly, pixel art, simple animations, and sparsely furnished scenes suggest that we are looking at a toy or, at least, a niche product.

If this view seems too simplistic or unjust, I agree. At the same time, my experience from working on both big and small titles taught me that if you want to fight for a bigger budget, to be taken seriously by investors and publishers, and then by players looking at the screenshots of your game on Steam, you have to deliver a certain look. The game needs to look "realistic."

I think that is the reason the phenomenal *Hellblade: Senua's Sacrifice* (a self-proclaimed *independent AAA*) is indeed treated as a small AAA game. It is not due to its length, gameplay, or themes, but to the fact that Senua's model and her facial animations look so naturalistic. Where it's important, the game looks like an AAA.

At the same time, a great turn-based role-playing game *Ruined King* set in the *League of Legends* franchise, a game much longer and with more complicated gameplay, is treated as non-AAA because, as one of the reviews stated, "less budget for story animation." With its graphic novel aesthetics, it just doesn't look like an AAA.

From the creator's perspective, it is easier to make your game look "real," especially if you work on one of the "big" game engines. At the moment I am writing this, if you want to make a 3D game, you can use Unity or the Unreal Engine. Both of those pieces of software come with everything you need to render beautiful graphics, simulate physics, move the character, play animations, etc. But, what's more important, in this context, both engines give you access to huge marketplaces, where you can buy ready-to-use art made by other professional users. War zones, city streets, deserts and forests, and dingy shantytowns are all just a click away.

Technologies that were cutting-edge or unheard of when I was starting my professional life are industry standards nowadays. Photo scans that can, with great visual fidelity, recreate almost any environment, motion-capture that brings more and more realistic movement to your characters, and AI-assisted asset generation that helps you make even more assets even faster. The technological landscape became a paradise for anyone making "realistic" games.

With every technological and conceptual improvement, we seem closer to reaching the ultimate goal: perfect realism, a simulation that is impossible to distinguish from the real thing. Because deep down, we—as players and as humans—expect that a world that looks real will behave like the real world. Also, some AAA games seem to answer our expectations. Just look at how real the rope behaves in *The Last of Us 2* or how true the world rings in the ultimate Wild West simulator *Read Dead Redemption 2*. Realism seems to rule supreme, at least in the AAA section of the market.

At the same time, when you are working on a smaller game, all those improvements and tools that help you make "realistic" games become a trap, because "realistic" games are all you can easily do. Just like with the legendary Ford Model T which came in any color the customer wished, so long as it was black. As easy as it is to find high-quality "realistic" graphical assets in the Unity or Unreal market-places, so hard it is to find assets that you can use in a game that deviates even a bit from the high visual fidelity paradigm. I learned it the hard way when a team I was a part of tried to quickly prototype in Unity a game with a very distinct visual style. We failed to deliver the visual production values required by the investors, because the asset store turned out to be all but useless, and our art team was too small to prepare the necessary models on time. Had we chosen a more "realistic" approach to the art style, things might have been different.

All chips seem to fall in favor of the high visual fidelity approach. Looking "real" is what people expect, it is what distinguishes the Big Boys from the Little League, and the technology, market, and infrastructure all make it quite easy to start making a "realistic" game.

But are realism, high visual fidelity, and the chase for the ultimate simulation the only way? Is it even a value we have to pursue as creators? I am not sure.

Quite the opposite in fact. I feel that we need all kinds of games, the "realistic" included, and I would be overjoyed if we—creators, players, and journalists—stopped treating them as the only way "real" games should present themselves. I might be preaching to a choir, but let me highlight some traps and consequences of the realistic approach.

I'll be frank—despite all the technological advances, I see the pursuit of "realistic graphics" as a wild goose chase, and one that takes a high toll on the artists engaged in the process. Every time a new version of a graphic card, or let's say, Unreal Engine comes out, and we see the demo, we are awestruck. We were not aware, up until that very moment, of how beautifully a game can look, how the light can play on the landscape, and how the multiple reflections and shimmering shadows can add to the atmosphere. As players or beginner developers, we begin expecting this level of visual fidelity as default.

But if we know a thing or two about making games, we realize that the law of diminishing returns is in play and that every increment toward the "truly realistic look" demands more and more effort. The textures have to be prepared in higher quality. The materials have to accommodate more and more parameters. Seems easy, but as I learned from a friend who is one of the best programmers specializing in lighting and rendering, is nothing but. Let's say you want a piece of wood to reflect light the way real wood does. To do that, you have to set all those parameters properly, which sometimes requires scanning the exact type of wood we want to simulate, which sometimes requires building a piece of hardware to do the scanning. The rabbit hole goes all the way down.

Motion-captured animations have to be cleaned by hand and incorporated into complicated behavior trees, photo scans need to be adjusted to fit the game, and all the new features highlighted in the demos eat all the memory leaving almost nothing for the actual game to run.

Preparing the underlying code also became more and more complicated, with tasks that a decade ago could be done by a mid-level specialist in a week, now taking an expert half a year to complete.

Details will vary, depending on the project, engine, and team, but the rule still applies. Every new shiny toy breeds myriad new tasks and requirements, and more and more people have to be engaged to prepare assets that would be compatible with the new features. As a result, every developer becomes just a cog in a machine and must accept that they may spend half a year making the light of a torch reflect from the environment the way it should, or a year and a half making sure that four-legged animals in the game traverse ramps in a believable way, or three years tweaking the material properties of all stones in the game. Soul crushing, at least for some.

The only reason that *The Last of Us 2* looked the way it looked was a team of 400 artists toiling away for years. The swelling of the teams is a fact you can't deny—the first Witcher was an AAA game when released, and the core team was about 60 people. Today, you can't even start production of an AAA without a team of 200. The sheer cost of hiring the team pushes big game companies toward repetitive low-risk projects. I will discuss more on that later.

Now, let's think for a moment about how we interact with games and in-game worlds. Every game is a new universe, with its unique set of rules. You could write a whole article just about this topic, and many people did. My favorite is Jonathan Blow's *The Witness*, which was—apart from being a philosophical essay—quite a good game. When we start playing any game, we immediately start learning what is possible and what is not possible within the boundaries of this particular world. In this learning process, we are being informed by two things: the explicit guidance provided by the game creators and our own general knowledge about the world.

Usually, after a tutorial and some trial and error, we learn what interactable objects look like, how far we can jump, etc. If we encounter a new situation, we first compare it to the known rules of the game, but if we can't do that, we assume what would happen, basing our assumptions on our general knowledge of the world. In other words, if we are not sure what the rules of the game are, we expect "realism," until proven otherwise.

In highly stylized games with a limited number of mechanics, this problem almost never exists. But in big, AAA titles, with high visual fidelity, everything pushes us into expecting the real thing. Let's take *Read Dead Redemption 2*, a game where your horse's balls shrink in the cold, and every game mechanic strives toward "realism." The game tells you to expect perfect simulation, and it usually delivers—but in contrast, the moments, when it doesn't, feel jarring. When we notice that train robberies play out in a dramatically different way during quests and in the open play, we are reminded by the imperfect simulation that this is not the Old West, but just a game. We feel cheated.

This promise of perfect simulation is an important by-product of striving for perfect visual fidelity. If everything we see behaves just like in the real world, if our character gets wet in the rain, leaves fall off a tree when we shake it, and light reflects off the water just like it should, we start believing that the whole world should behave "realistically." And our expectations extend to the game mechanics. We expect to be able to solve every problem in any way that seems "realistic" to us. We expect the game world to behave just like our real world.

For me, as a designer, the thought of perfect simulation is a nightmare—a very exciting nightmare but a nightmare nonetheless. With every step toward the perfect simulation, the complexity of the design, and the needed manpower increase exponentially (or at least significantly). The question of whether the needed complexity translates to interesting design is another matter. And, no matter how well you would do your job, there always would be that one player, who defined what is realistic differently than the design team did.

You can notice that the best immersive sims use stylized graphics and a set of clearly defined powers and mechanisms. They very clearly explain the boundaries of "realism" and present a finite set of tools you can use to solve puzzles in a very controlled environment. The player's agency and the feeling that you can do anything is based on a clear set of constraints, not on a perfect, unbounded simulation.

Let's consider this question: Is the perfect simulation of everything, of every step, every item, and every action a value? My personal opinion is that no, it is not.

Let's take a look at more established media. Movies do not show every second of the characters' lives and do not focus on each and every little thing, because it doesn't serve the experience. Movies are equally made by what was cut as by what was shown on screen. And if a movie is shot in one take, that is because of a conscious artistic decision, and not because the public expects "realism." Similarly in our medium, only certain genres of games need simulation, while in others, striving for perfect simulation would hurt the experience.

Unity of action, time, and place was a hit—in ancient Greece. Why do we try to impose such an anachronic approach to such a new and exciting medium as games? This is a tongue-in-the-cheek question, but I felt the need to ask it anyway.

So, is high visual fidelity a must? Can we only engage emotionally with games that are realistic? That this is not the case, especially if you are from my generation, or you collect retro game consoles. Because the pixelated, visually simplified games of my childhood were very engaging indeed. Many of them still are—playing Mario on a retro Gameboy is still fun. Of course, some types of gameplay have matured and changed a lot since I was a kid, so enjoying them today is hard, and sometimes impossible. But the main obstacle, in my experience, is not the quality of the graphics, but the clunkiness of the UX. As far as the visual side is concerned, games that got old the least gracefully are those who strived for "realistic" graphics at their release. By today's standards, Gameboy Mario is cool because it's retro, while *The Witcher* from 2007 is just ugly.

I think that as the game engines' capacity to simulate reality increases, older and older games will slide into this aesthetic uncanny valley, where "realistic" becomes "ugly." The bar moves higher and higher with every iteration of software and hardware, and with it, the game budgets and team sizes swell. Higher "realism" levels mean higher budgets, higher budgets mean higher risk, and higher risk means less innovation. Over just two console generations, the costs of making AAA games skyrocketed. The first Witcher game cost about 4 million dollars to produce, with *The Witcher 3* the cost rose to 13 million dollars, while the cost of making *Cyberpunk 2077* amounted to 178 million dollars. The most visible effect of this vicious circle of rising costs and risk aversion is mainstream game series, where new installments look better but offer virtually the same gameplay as their ancestors. They are, in a way, just better-looking reskins, and the increase in visual fidelity is smaller with every new installment.

The closer games are to "realistic" graphics, the more similar they look. It's no wonder, as they all aim at exactly the same point—the real-world look. The process is accelerated by the creeping monopolization of the game engine market. More and more studios find it too risky or too expensive to maintain their own engines, and constantly upgrade their rendering, physics engines, liquid and cloth simulation, etc. It is easier to use the industry's golden standard, which is, at least today, the Unreal Engine.

An example from another industry comes to mind. In 1934, Kodak introduced format 135—a type of 35-mm film, designed for photography, perforated with Kodak Standard perforations. By the late 1960s, it became the most popular photographic film size and remains the most popular film size today. And just like, for many years, the Kodak film shaped the look of our photographs, the Unreal Engine is beginning to shape the look of our games. It's harder and harder for mainstream games to find their own look. Because how can you find your own, unique style, when you try to mimic the same thing, using the same tools, as dozens of other game studios?

When we look at the history of art, we notice that all visual arts had their period of striving toward visual fidelity. In European painting, we could say it started during the Italian Renaissance, with the discovery of linear perspective. Since that moment, striving for "realism" (and perspective-based visual illusions) has become something of value. Visual fidelity was hard to achieve, so it became the field where artists could flaunt their skill, prove their mastery, and justify the cost of their work. Similarly to games, this process also involved technology. The Dutch Masters, famous for their photorealistic paintings, used *camera obscura* to capture the finest details. And it was technology that ended the race toward realism. With the discovery and popularization of photography, capturing reality-as-it-was ceased to be a sign of mastery. Everyone could do it. The perspective shifted, and the demands of the public shifted as well. The artist was no longer supposed to replicate reality, but to infuse it with emotions, and meanings, and even deform it in an intriguing way. In painting, realism gave way to impressionism, cubism, and abstraction. In sculpture, we find Auguste Rodin's unique style more interesting than earlier, mimetic works of other artists. We started to appreciate works of art that represented not the outside, real world, but shed light on the inside worlds of a human observer.

I don't think that realism is a great way of making artistic statements. Or, at least, it is not an easy way of making that. Let's take into consideration James Cameron's *Avatar*, a beautiful movie with a surprisingly small fandom. Visually stunning, with the most realistic approach to 3D cinema to date, it seems to lack something that ignites the viewer's imagination. I am still not sure whether the Na'vi are an artistic statement, or am I supposed to believe that they are a product of evolution happening on a planet far away? I drink in the views but remain emotionally distant.

This is a highly subjective view, but I have a similar problem, with games that merge overly familiar gameplay with visually stunning "realistic" graphics. As soon as I realize where the boundaries of the game world are, all the work of the hundreds of artists becomes transparent to me. I filter out the "decorations" and only see the function of objects: This is an enemy, this is a path forward, this is a puzzle, and this is a quest-giver. Emotionally, I stop caring for how they look because they look "normal." When things look in a game like they look by default, there's no longer anything special about them.

Compared to games with "realistic" graphics, heavily stylized characters in the Dishonored series, the simple yet beautiful vistas of Journey, the cell-shaded desert of Sable, or the surreal graphics of *Kentucky Road Zero* make a much stronger impression on me. The way objects in the game world look, bears meaning, says something about the setting, makes me think, and inspires a moment of reflection.

Personally, both as a player and a designer, I prefer games with stylized graphics. I have my reasons. When I stylize I can make statements. When I stylize I don't have to simulate everything. When I stylize we don't need over a thousand people to make a game.

Personally, I would love the industry to—not pivot away from realism, which would be unrealistic—but acknowledge games that break out from the mold of "realism" and use their visual language to make a statement. To open to the possibility, the games with stylized graphics and curated mechanics can also be treated as AAA.

Perhaps I would like to see less mimicry and more art.

5

AUTHORIAL VOICE AND INTENT IN SYSTEM DESIGN

MARTA FIJAK

Authorial voice, in literature, refers to the unique style and tone that an author uses to convey their perspectives, opinions, and ideas in their writing. It is their fingerprint on the work they create. A mark that it was made by a human. Clear evidence of human-to-human communication—not an encyclopedic entry that just lists facts*, redacted and approved by a lot of people to erase any single human touch. This *authorial voice* is not unique to literature. It is present in all expressions of human creativity. Does not matter if it's music, film, book, or a painting. The voice is characteristic of the given creator, shaped by their personal experiences, cultural backgrounds, approach to their craft, etc.

> * In the world that we are living in, many things tell us that they are just a statement of facts, unbiased. Many of those things are lying to us. Even if the factual content is true, the act of omission of some facts and bolding of others is an authorial intent in itself. Sometimes it is unconscious. In academia, this is solved by coauthorship and a rigorous reviewing process, but this discussion is far outside the scope of this book.

Emanations of authorial voice can be unintentional. Frankly, they mostly are, as understanding our own style and perspective comes with experience and mature auto-reflection about the process of creation. Still, even with less experienced creators, this authorial voice is present—it may be not so coherent or underdeveloped, but still, it is there. You cannot create without an authorial voice—intentional or not.

 DOI: 10.1201/9781003325031-5

Authorial intent is different—the word intent suggests a conscious decision. We want to communicate something—a fantasy, a statement, a critique—this is our intent. Even in a capitalistic setup, where the base reason for the creation of many things is generating profit, there is still lower level intent—the fantasy, the topic, the story that we want to tell. Yes, there will be changes based on market research, budget, and target audience, but still, it's hard to create without the intent to communicate. At least, theoretically, it should be this way, but we've probably all seen the development hell of incoherent vision and lack of clear intent*.

> * It's a huge topic (that I also have scars from), but many times, big productions with great teams behind them fail due to (among other things) the lack of coherent vision of what they are making—an article about Anthem written by Jason Schreier is a good starting point.

For literature (or solo-music acts), this authorial voice and intent are of a single person. They shape every little aspect of the creation according to the rules of their craft. They make millions of decisions along the way. Those decisions vary in scope and impact on the creation. Let's look at the high-impact decision on the example of two books about war: "Catch-22" by J. Heller and "Band of Brothers" by Stephen E. Ambrose. Both of them tell stories about soldiers during World War II. Yet, those books couldn't be more different. One is a take on chaos and the lack of sense in war. The second one is a celebration of the bravery of soldiers and the camaraderie between them. This is an example of the manifestation of authorial voice and intent: both of those authors made a conscious* decision on how they depicted war. After this grand decision, a set of smaller, some con-

> * Or not. I do not know those gentlemen personally.

scious, some unconscious decisions followed. What characters to include, what scenes to add, and even what words to use? All of that gives us vastly distinct books, yet the core element they depict, war, is the same.

Movies and games are slightly different*. They are a choir of authorial voices, as the teams responsible for them can be hundreds of people. Those voices can harmonize with each other, but they can also

* Here, we are talking about more mainstream productions. Solo games or indie films operate more like books. The body of works of Lukas Pope or Benedict Foddy comes to mind.

create a cacophony of sounds. It's all up to the choir conductor to make something beautiful out of all of this—this can be a game director, movie director, executive producer, etc. Their authorial voice and intent guide all of the other ones*. Still, this authorial voice of many people is present in those bigger creations, so yes, games also. It is present on every level of the creation,

* It is described in detail in Chapter 9.

and it comes from every team member. Depending on the position of the team member on the ladder of any sort, it may be more or less prominent in the creation, but it is still there.

Let's dissect how this authorial voice and intent gets expressed in games. First, in those places that are obvious and usually conscious. Later, let's look at a way of expressing that is usually overlooked in terms of communication and instead seen as a way of creating engagement—mechanics. Because, yes, those are also manifestations of intent marked with unique authorial voices. It's important to be aware of that because revealing ourselves in places where we think that we are not speaking can be problematic. In the best case, we will create a bunch of things that are hard to understand. In the medium case, the game won't be coherent (and the authorial intent will be all over the place), and in extreme cases, we will say something very unintended/problematic/wrong or just plainly evil. Long story short we need to discuss system rhetorics.

Before we jump into that big jar of pickles*, let's get into the things that we have in common with other mediums—the triforce: The plot, art, and music—more or less, the static elements of narration*. For these three, we have a platter of theories and resources from which we can

* System rhetorics, just restating it for clarity.

* It is described in Chapter 6.

learn how to express ourselves. When those things are coherent, magic happens—let's take, for example, *This War of Mine* (2014) by 11 bit studios. The game's intent is to present the human toll of armed conflicts.

* Loosely inspired by the Siege of Sarajevo.

The story revolves around a group of civilians trying to survive in a besieged city*. The game is grim and serious in tone, and it is expressed in the triforce. The story bits show the hardship of survival and the sacrifices you've got to make. They also build the topic of war, with classic imagery of soldiers, looters, pain, and things that got lost. On the visual side, the game operates on a dim, almost black-and-white palette, with splashes of unfriendly blue, dim yellow, and sickly green. It is aesthetic and conscious in its visual design but depressing. Instead of character portraits, there are photos of real people—not glamorous ones, but ordinary, like you and me*.

* Those are photos of team members, friends, and people who worked in the same building where 11 bit studios was located back then.

The audio design is naturalistic, and the music is calm and nostalgic, with splashes of something more when characters are listening to the radio—a Polish punk/alternative rock band that gives the game its placement*. Not America, but something closer to Eastern Europe. All of those things create a coherent expression of the given intent, shaped by the unique voice of creators*.

* To be precise, a Polish band called Cool Kids of Death.

* It is an interesting thought experiment: To imagine this game (or any other) made by developers from an entirely different culture.

In a perfect world, all of the decisions that we make are at least semi-conscious. We make a given character a villain because it makes sense for the story and themes and not because of internal bias. We use Dutch angle to create unease in the player*, not because we feel the

* It is a way of framing where the frame is tilted, creating a sense of unease and disorientation in the viewer. *12 Monkeys* (1995) has a ton of such shots.

unease with the content of the frame. We pick color schemes to invoke certain historical connotations or emotions. This is not a matter of auto policing and being correct but the ability to convey a strong intent when creating in our unique style. As creators, each one of us is responsible for what we are saying, so it is good to know that we are saying something and not doing it unintentionally. Outside of personal expression, this intent gives us more coherent experiences for the player*.

Ok, so now the obvious means of expression for the author's intent and voice are out of our way. Let's jump into the previously mentioned jar of pickles—mechanics. To call it fancier, this jar of pickles is called system rhetorics*. Before we dwell deeper, let's agree on a set of definitions:

* Sometimes, the goal of the experience could be the contrast—at first glance, to work does not seem coherent. Creating the effect consciously differentiates it from random noise. Players can feel the difference.

* A very similar approach was suggested by a game studies author, Ian Bogost, in 2006 in his book *Persuasive Games: The Expressive Power of Videogames*, where he introduces a concept of procedural rhetorics.

- **Mechanic**—the basic building component of gameplay, rules that define what actions a player can perform and what is the response of the game, i.e. a running mechanic (when the player moves the analog stick forward, the character accelerates in a given direction, with speed described as a curve dependent on time).
- **System**—a shorthand to talk about groups of mechanics that are closely intertwined, i.e. movement system (moving mechanic, jumping mechanic, ducking mechanic, and sliding mechanic).
- **System rhetoric**—how the system conveys meaning to inform, persuade, or take a stance on a given subject. What the rules in place communicate, and what the dynamics coming out of them say. A space in which authorial intent and voice are expressed.

To conceptualize those things in motion, we will rely on a butchered version of the Mechanics-Dynamics-Aesthetics framework (MDA). Butchering, in this case, is just taking the basic elements of the framework, simplifying them, and ignoring the controversial part*. The MDA conceptualizes gameplay as a communication between the designer and the player in the following way: We have a mechanic that, when put

* The controversial part, in this case, is the list of different sources for the Aesthetic element of the MDA model. This part won't be needed for our analysis, though.

in motion (by both simulation itself and the player interaction), generates a dynamic, which is perceived by the player in the form of aesthetic. So system rhetoric focuses on analyzing and shaping meaning embedded in those two first elements of the MDA model.

Here also lies the old and already dismantled ludo narrative dissonance. With this model and definitions, we can frame it as system rhetorics stating something different than the static narration elements—clean and simple.

All is nice and clean at a high level of abstraction*, but there are a few things to dis-

* At least, I hope so.

mantle here—first is how the gameplay speaks, and what do we mean by stating that the system says something—how they express this authorial voice and intent. The second part is cultural literacy, aka do players read systems and absorb the meaning coming out of them, or is this layer entirely ignored? And as always, a third layer, they question why we, as developers, should care about all of that.

Let's start with a very basic example of a mechanic speaking. Let's say that I'm designing a weapon system. Plain and simple, some components to put together and fill up with numbers to create different types of guns, swords, etc. I can sit down now and write down the specifications. By doing that, I will communicate one thing to you about me very strongly—I have absolutely no idea about firearms. What are recoil and bullet spread? No idea. So it will leave a gap in my design, and those things won't be present. Worse, not present not as an intent (as it makes sense to leave those out in a fast-paced arcade shooter) but as a blind spot—I have no idea that those things exist*. I'm telling you that to you in

* Please ignore the fact that I just wrote about a thing that I don't know if exists at all—just roll with it for the sake of the example.

my design. Of course, this is a clear-cut example, and with one simple trick, it can be solved—research. I believe that research is second nature to all designers, so that we can consciously decide which part of real-life inspirations we want to put into our designs and which we want to omit (and for what reason!). Still, if this landed in the game, it would cause a hurdle for the player to learn the game. They come with a preconceived notion of what a weapon is, how weapons behave, etc. Yet, the systems in this world say something different—there may be a reason for that, sure, but this should not happen by accident.

Ok, so let's complicate the example. I wake up one morning, and boom, I'm working on *Frostpunk* again*. I need to create a set of new laws. One of them is a law allowing immigration to our last city on Earth*. I know that each law has to have a positive effect and

> * *Frostpunk* (2018) is a society survival city-builder game, serious in its tone and the depiction of rather adult themes.

> * Don't ask from where those people are migrating.

a negative effect. A form of trade-off for the player, so enacting a law was not a trivial decision but something with meaningful consequences for further play. Ok, so positives, yup, more workers (as lack of people is always a problem in *Frostpunk*), but what is the explicit downside to it? Yes, more people always sink more resources, but that is true for every increase in the population, so what would be something unique to this law? There are many options. It can be a rise of discontent. It can be a rise in the crime rate. It may be a set of new unique demands coming from the immigrants. It can be even some new system depicting tensions between old citizens and new citizens. There are dozens of ideas that would fulfill the design purpose of this feature. So which one is the correct one? The trick is, there is no right answer. Yes, doing research will generate a big set of very different, sometimes contradicting, pros and cons. Which one will you pick, if not examined, will be just a reflection of your inner stance on this real-world issue. Stating that immigrants have unique demands is a vastly different world view that staying they increase the crime rate. The one you pick will be the one that feels right for you, and that "makes sense." This "making sense" is you speaking through the design—it's good to be conscious about it. So how to pick "the set?" That's the authorial intent part—you want to say something about this society, how they would react, what kind of people they are, etc. Examining it from this perspective may offer a more coherent experience in the broad terms of the game*.

* There is a trick, though, as this intent usually comes from higher up, a game director, etc. You might not agree with what they are trying to say. It's a non-trivial problem that we explore in depth in Chapter 9.

We can even go deeper because systems in games don't exist without their content, i.e. variable values, so we know how much gold is produced, how much damage is received, etc. We understand it instinctively, as this is the bread and butter of survival and horror games. Many of them are built around scarcity. The tension comes from it—the lack of ammo, low health, spare batteries for the flashlight, etc. Those values communicate to the player that this is a tough situation, they build cohesion in the experience, and they guide the player toward the intended playstyle. Numbers express things and communicate things—gaining levels represent the growth of a character, different damage values represent different sizes of threats, etc. There are also less obvious examples, such as probabilities in *Rimworld* for the sexual orientation of pawns[1]—Simone de Rochefort summed it up nicely in a *Polygon* article (2016) in a sentence, *"You can't create a system for sexuality without sharing your thoughts on sex."* What is interesting in that case is the fact that this discussion was sparked by the players—this will tie nicely to the topic of players' literacy and understanding system rhetorics in a few paragraphs later.

Before we get there, let's take one more final example of an authorial voice in system design: *Tetris*. Yes, those tetrominoes that slide down the screen to form lines and disappear together. What is this system expressing? Jenet Murey[2] suggested that *Tetris* is a depiction of an overburdened American worker in the 90s*, constantly under the pressure of new tasks that need to be placed in an already busy schedule. Too much? Yeah,

* Even though it's a Russian game from the 80s.

definitely, at least for me. This was an extreme interpretation during the war between ludologist and narratologist in the Game Studies land*. The thing is, the further a system is an abstraction, the broader the scope of interpretations. From the game

> * OK, war is too strong of a word. It was a prolonged discussion about the nature of games and how to interpret them as part of culture.

development approach to system rhetorics, it just shows that some systems don't say anything meaningful to the broader group of players, and that is ok.

The idea here is that the closer you are to reality in your game, the more important is the rhetoric of the system. Most games are still pretty close though, as this clause applies mostly to abstract logic games that are not narrative experiences in any form*. When I say close to reality, I do not mean Earth, 2023, I rather mean that at least some rules of our world apply to the

> * Like most of Zachtronics games where a residual story is present only to offer the game a structure, and it's absolutely not necessary.

world inside of the game. It can be physics, social interactions, or even the mere existence of characters. So, if you base the game on reality, it is an expression of your view of reality—it will show as an emanation of your authorial voice.

Now we know that systems say something—the other part of the equation is, is anybody listening? A long story short, it depends. The previous example of *Rimworld* shows that, yes, people can read system rhetorics. On the other hand, we have *The Sims* (2000). On the systems' rhetoric level, this game is a critique of the consumerism lifestyle. Don't believe me? Here is an excerpt from an interview given by Will Wright:

> *On the surface, The Sims is meant to be a kind of parody of consumerism. Every object you buy in the game has a potential failure state. It can get dirty or break or need to be taken out with the trash or whatever. All the objects are saying, 'Buy me! Buy me! I'll make you happy. I'll save you time. But if you play the game in that way and build a big mansion full of all these cool plasma TVs and hot tubs and stuff, you'll find at some point that something's always going wrong, and the Sims are running around having to deal with*

maintaining the objects. The game is tooled so that they promise to save you time but beyond some point they actually become a huge time sink.[3]

Nowadays, the Wikipedia article about all *Sims* game installments is a few pages long, full of expansions and new stuff that you can get for your Sim. Just buy, buy, buy, and express yourself. The intended meaning was also slowly washed away from the game, with difficulty known from the first installment disappearing and breaking down and repairing mechanics being less and less punishing. Why did all of this happen? Was it due to not strongly enough expressed authorial intent of the first one, or was it due to immense success and the possibility of a long-lasting franchise with huge profit? Your guess is as good as mine*.

* OK, we all know the answer.

Another story that comes to mind is the story of the board game Monopoly. Have you ever played it? Have you enjoyed it on its mechanical level? Or the main appeal was the fury of your friends when after the first hour, you were the biggest owner, and you just bathed in their misery, as they paid and paid and had no way to catch up with you? From my anecdotal evidence, it's about slowly sipping on the tears of your enemies while you clean your monocle and position the top hat just right. Board games purists will say it's just not a good game—it allows a snowball effect* —when you get an advantage early on, it

* In design terms, there is a positive feedback loop.

will just multiply, and no one can threaten the winning player's position.

The fun part, and for many years forgotten, is that it is like that by design. The game was created by Elizabeth Magie, at the beginning of the 20th century, to showcase the economic consequences of Ricardo's Law of Economic Rent and the Georgist concepts of economic privilege and land value taxation.[4] Long story short, it plays this "poorly" by design. The authorial intent is to show the snowball effect. It's a teaching tool that allows us to feel the abstract economic concept on our own skin. How this intended meaning was lost in history, we already know, with Monopoly being one of the biggest board game franchises of all time, with thematic editions that hide the intended meaning even further. The message is even harder to read if, instead of real estate, you are playing with Pokemon characters, Game of Thrones lands, or just plain and simple cats. There is even a World War II edition with a lovely text on the box—*"Wheel and deal World War II events such as Pearl Harbor, D-Day Normandy and Battle of the Bulge in an effort to own these momentous pieces of history."*

Are those two examples a guideline to just skip the system rhetorics entirely? I see them more as a cautionary tale—pure mechanics, without the strong support of static elements (texts, pictures, etc.), are hard to read by broader audiences. They can be read instead as unintentional, or just plain bad game design. As always, everything speaks in context. On the other hand, if the context is provided, even the most frustrating* mechanics can work very nicely to underline the intent.

* In a classic sense, like repetitive or unjust for the player.

There are more, let's say, adventurous examples of this strong system rhetorics—i.e. *Pathologic 2* (2019)*. A game where you are a doctor, returning to a very peculiar village that is going to be struck by a pandemic. The survival mechanics in the game are brutal.

* I'm aware that the release dates, the relation between *Pathologic* and *Pathologic 2*, etc., are a convoluted story on its own—for the sake of clarity, let's go with the English language release on Steam—*Pathologic 2*.

From the get-go, hunger forces you to scavenge through garbage cans, and the combat is the antithesis of power fantasy—it's sluggish and unresponsive. On top of that, the reputation system makes even exploration a huge hustle, as everybody hates you. Oh and did I tell you that the player has no idea what's happening and little to no guidance? Without the context of the whole game, we could say that this is just plain bad design. Yet, the game has a very positive rating on Steam (with more than 6k reviews at the time of writing), a strong 8.8 user reviews (303 ratings), and 70 Metacritic from reviewers*. Plus, there are

* Which makes a lot of sense, as the game is highly unsuitable for tight review deadlines.

YouTube videos with millions of views*, praising why this game is genius. Players praise those odd design choices, as the intent of the whole experience is felt in every inch of this game. The narrative of the game would not play out as strongly if the static elements were the same, but the dynamic ones were fun. It's

> * The hbomberguy video has 7.7 million views at the moment, and it is two hours long. Yes, it is based on *Pathologic*, not *Pathologic 2*, but *Pathologic* is *Pathologic 2*, kind of. Don't get me started on how convoluted the history of this game is. TL;DR *Pathologic 2* is part of *Pathologic 1* but done better and in English. More or less.

an extreme example of system rhetorics supporting the whole experience so strongly. It also makes the game a niche product, but still, players who are interested in less orthodox experiences understand it and love it.

Yet, to communicate through systems, we don't have to go so far. The plain cohesion of what systems say and what static elements say elevates the experience*, and decreases the cognitive burden for the player, as the narrative in all elements tells the same story. There is of course a trick

> * What happens if they don't work together is described in Chapter 6— the story of Lara and the deer.

to all of this, as mechanics play a dual role in games. Not only those are parts of the narration (and as such, they represent authorial intent and voice) they are also there to create interesting decision spaces on every loop level. Sometimes those two aspects do not go well together. Is one more inherently important than the other? I would say no. Everything depends on the game that is being created. What is the key aspect of it, what the vision document says, and what is the intent of the whole thing? Is it creating a playful space for the player to explore or to tell a morally ambiguous story? Games are always some form of abstraction, representing things in a simplified (from a system perspective), interactive way. What is simplified and in what way but still supporting themes, and what is simplified is that the inspiration is unrecognizable—at first glance, it says nothing is up to the creator—what's important is for that to be a conscious decision.

We are humans, and as such, everything we create has our own authorial voice embedded in it and is created with some kind of authorial intent. It is also true for systems, so it's our responsibility to do it deliberately and consciously, revealing what we want about ourselves, telling what we intend to say, and, at the end of the day, creating cohesive and moving experiences for the player.

Notes

1 There is a *Polygon* article discussing it in broader terms: https://www.polygon.com/2016/11/4/13529134/sexuality-in-rimworld
2 J. Murray, *Hamlet on the Holodeck: the Future of Narrative in Cyberspace.*
3 From an interview given to *Telegraph Magazine* in 2004: https://www.smh.com.au/technology/sims-like-us-20041218-gdkc7w.html
4 David Parlett (1999). *The Oxford History of Board Games.* Oxford University Press. p. 352. ISBN 0-19-212998-8.

6
The Topography
of Narrative

MARTA FIJAK

Let's start with the obvious. Games tell stories. Sometimes those are convoluted epics that require a whiteboard and a dedicated fanbase to understand them fully*, and sometimes they are as simple as a miraculous victory by getting that straight tetromino in

---
* I'm looking at you, *Kingdom Hearts* and *Metal Gear Solid*.
---

a tense game of *Tetris*. Nonetheless, games are a storytelling medium, a unique one, as the player is a co-author of the story.

Sure, we can say that this is not as special as we think it is, as Umberto Eco created the term *textual cooperation* many years ago. It is a concept that describes the vital role of the reader in creating the meaning of a book, but games invite the player to coauthor the story on a deeper level. Not only the level of interpretation but also picking and shaping the experience they are going to have. Of course, this shaping is, in a way, smoke and mirrors, a parlor trick, as the choices that the player makes are still bound by the options provided by the developer. Different games offer different degrees of freedom. This greatly affects how the story is told and even what kind of story can be told.

Before we dive into what that means exactly, a clean-up of vocabulary is needed. Games are complex beasts of many moving parts and depending on who you ask, those parts are named differently. To ensure that we are on the same page, I will use the following approach:

- **Narration**—a single story experienced by the player in a single playthrough. It is created as a sum of dynamic and static story elements.

DOI: 10.1201/9781003325031-6

- **Static elements**—all things that will always be the same, from player to player; so, all cutscenes, all written dialogues, characters, events, etc. Of course, their meaning may be changed by context, but their content is always the same, and they carry some information on their own*.

  * There may be some slight procedural variation in the prewritten text, like adding the player's name—this I treat as a static element. On the other hand, procedurally generated text, like the one present in *Curious Expedition*, for example, escapes this definition, as those text fragments from which a given text is constructed don't have a lot of meaning on their own.

- **Dynamic elements**—elements that come out as an effect of the player engaging with the mechanics. They can change the context of static elements but, on their own, only carry a little storytelling information.

We can map relationships between those elements to give us a clearer overview of what is happening when narration is created in the mind of the player.

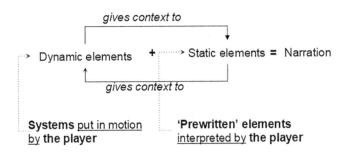

In this chapter, let's focus on the relation and ratio between those static and dynamic elements and how they impact both development and the possible narration*.

* This graph also implies a vital role of system rhetorics, co-authorship, player background, etc. We explore those topics in a different chapter.

With those loose definitions and the flowchart under our belt, let's analyze narrations created by two games: *Civilization VI* and *Life is Strange*.

In broad terms, the *narration* depicts a civilization rising to power. It has twists and turns, moments of sudden betrayals, devastating wars, successful peace talks, and technological progress or religious domination. Yet, those stories come primarily out of *dynamic* elements: the resources management, diplomacy, combat systems, etc., which are put in motion by the player. Without long chains of player actions, the story falls apart. At least the story of their empire, as AI will play the parts of that story on their own (but not in a static sense!).

On the other hand, we have *Life is Strange*, a *narration* about friendship, growing up, the consequences of our actions, and living with them. This story is guided by the player, but not as strongly coauthored as the *Civilization* playthrough was. The *dynamic* elements focus on allowing the player to explore the static elements. The player walking and rewinding time is necessary for the creation of the narration but not crucial in terms of shaping it. It can give a slightly different context to the *static* elements that the player witnesses but does not dramatically change the meaning. It does not mean that the player does not dramatically impact the narration. They do, but in strictly predefined moments in time, where the player picks from strict *static* choices of significant consequences.

To be clear, this differentiation is not a statement of judgment. One is not more of a game than another, nor is one inherently better than another. Those two games just use different mixes of the means that games offer as a storytelling medium. Yet, the ratio between *static* and *dynamic* elements has significant consequences for the narrative that the game offers. It puts different traps and possibilities, aims at different types of players, and even impacts the budget of a production, as different rations have different *expected qualities*. But let's not get ahead of ourselves; first, we need to examine closely how those dynamic elements impact the narration, especially since it is a little bit more tricky than how a prewritten dialogue fragment or a cutscene does it.

Again, as games are complicated beasts of many moving parts, we need to build a common playing field for conceptualizing dynamic elements. For the sake of this chapter, I will rely on Brian Upton's definition of games, supporting it with loop definitions by Michael

Sellers. If you are familiar with those frameworks, feel free to skip the next few paragraphs, as I'm going to summarize them (and probably slightly butcher them for the sake of simplicity).

There are a multitude of game definitions. Some describe what they are like, for example, the classical definition by J. Huizinga stated in Homo Ludens*. Some, on the other hand, explain what they do, like the J. Schell one, stated in *The Art of Game Design: The Book of Lenses*. Both descriptive and functional definitions are useful tools to use while designing. Here let's go with one of the functional definitions—B. Upton's one stated in *Aesthetic of Play* (2008). It says that: "a game is a free movement in a system of constraints." It sounds obvious but is paired with the framework for conceptualizing a game as a set of states, which will be helpful in the dissection of narration creation in games. So let's explore this, using every game designer's favorite example: Chess.

* This definition goes as follows: "Play is a free activity standing quite consciously outside 'ordinary' life as being 'not serious,' but at the same time absorbing the player intensely and utterly. It is an activity connected with no material interest, and no profit can be gained by it. It proceeds within its own proper boundaries of time and space according to fixed rules and in an orderly manner."

* This one looks like this: "a game is a problem-solving activity, approached with a playful attitude."

As a state in chess, we take the literal state of the board, so what pieces are left on the board, and where they are. For simplicity, we will remove the current emotional state of the players from the equation. The system of constraints in this situation is the set of chess rules, starting from the size of the board, through the number of chess pieces, and ending on the game's turn-based nature. The player, by their actions, can change the state of the game, but they can only change it to another state that is valid in the constraints created by the rules of the game. So we can now imagine the whole game of chess as a set of transitions from state to state. Of course, from every single state, we can go to many different states, but here comes the player and their anticipatory play. The player wants to get to the state where they win, so they imagine the best path going through different states to get to that point. However, there is a problem, in the form of the other player, who, with every move of their own, changes the state of the game. This changes the path our player has imagined and forces them to adapt.

To sum up, all of the systems and mechanics in place create both all of the possible states in a game but also all of the possible transitions*. As we go on, an example of Civilization, both those states and transitions can be a powerful storytelling device, but let's not get ahead of ourselves—especially since we have one more layer of foundations to lay down in the form of a different perspective of the game experience—the loops!

Loops are the bread and butter of design and one of the fundamental approaches to examining games*. Establishing an engaging core loop is one of the first things to do when starting a preproduction of a project. Yet thinking about only the core loop may be misleading, as it implies the existence of one loop to rule them all—the most important one etc. Games are constructed of many loops that together create the structure of the experience for the player. To structure those loops in a way that will allow clear communication, let's rely on the division proposed by M. Sellers in *Advanced Game Design: A Systems Approach* (2017). The division goes as follows:

* We can conceptualize every game in that way, but analyzing every single state is usually counterproductive, as games like FIFA, i.e. have an infinite number of states from the perspective of our slimy brains. Still, we can aim to create a designed set of states and incentivize the player to transition between them in a way that we, the designers, see as the best for the experience.

* But it's not a "one fits all" solution, especially when examining more narratively stiff games—walking sims, point and clicks, etc. Sure, you can write them inside of the loop, but it usually is an exercise for the sake of an exercise and does not offer any deeper form of understanding.

- **Action feedback loop**—an extremely short form of a loop that can be summed up in a sentence "click and something happens," e.g. first-person shooter combat heavily relies on that kind of loop, and rhythm games are almost entirely constructed out of it.

- **Short-term cognitive loop**—a loop that involves conscious planning and engagement of something more than pure reflex. It may be creating another batch of soldiers in an RTS game to destroy the enemy's tanks or planning a route in an FPS game to the closest ammo pack.
- **Long-term cognitive loop**—a more cognitively strenuous and longer version of the previous one. It consists of long-term plans and goals, such as shaping the character by using a progression system in a cRPG or optimizing toward technological victory in a game of Civilization.
- **Emotional loop**—a loop that moves away from purely cognitive goals and plans and moves the play space into more emotional territory. Every time we design with the intention that emotions will be important, and not only min-maxing when players make a decision, we use emotional loops. All decisions that have, e.g. a moral weight will be there—like most of the decisions in *Papers, Please*.
- **Cultural loop**—a loop that happens mostly outside of the game. This is the cultural discussion and context of how the game is played and if it is played at all. An example here would be a game called *Trains* by B. Romers. After understanding what the game is about, the act of further playing or leaving the table is a part of this play space*.

* In this tabletop game, players are responsible for putting little yellow people on trains. The game, at the beginning, does not state where those yellow people are going. You just try to put in as many as you can, and then the reveal comes. Those trains are going to a concentration camp, and those little yellow people represent Jews. Whether you decide to change your goal in the game, or stop playing altogether, is a part of the game itself.

Not every game focuses on every type of loop, furthermore, not every game has every type of loop. Where *Stellaris* mostly plays out on a long-term cognitive loop, the *Guitar Hero* games are almost purely an action-feedback loop. In the same way, different games create the key elements of their narrations on different loops. Different loops also create different goals for the player that motivate them to transition between game states and put the end goal in a set of nicer, manageable steps. Taking that all in, let's take it into practice and look at two examples: *Rimworld* and *Hellblade*.

Let me tell you a story about a chicken. A multitude of them, to be precise. The game in which it happened was *Rimworld*—a top-down colony sim game where the player's purpose is to ensure the survival and prosperity of a small group of people stranded on a distant planet.

My colony was small, just four people, in dire shape and with grim prospects. Winter was just starting, and our food stockpiles were almost empty. With the lack of hunting animals, starvation was imminent. Yet a small miracle has happened, a radio transmission informing us about a lost cargo, not far away from us, full of chickens—six of them, to be precise. Hope has risen. A plan was hatched. I divided my people into two groups. One would go on a dangerous adventure to save the chickens and bring them back to the colony. The second would, in the meantime, build the best coop the world has ever seen. Heating, some hay bought from merchants, and a roof over chickens' heads. Everything to ensure that those sweet, sweet eggs would allow everyone to survive the harsh conditions that came upon us all.

Of course, this is *Rimworld*. If something can go wrong, it will. My away team got ambushed by bandits. One of my men was killed, another badly wounded. Still, the life of the other two colonists was at stake, so with the last effort, this colonist, almost on the edge of death, brought the box full of chickens home.

The home team was not better. An electric circuit shorted, setting parts of the base on fire. Those left behind extinguished it but got severely burned. Still, through pain, they finished building the coop. Everything for the sweet, sweet eggs.

The wonderful moment has come. The surviving three of them stood around the box to witness the chickens enter their new home. Yet, when the animals got released, the hope disappeared (especially for me, as AI in games is not there yet). Yes, there were six of them, but they were all roosters. Six roosters, not enough to survive the winter and with no chance for eggs.

All of my colonists were dead in a matter of the next few weeks, but before that happened, there was a feast with a wonderful rooster soup as the main course.

Of course, I took some liberties when retelling this story, but still, it has happened to me. The probability that it has happened to another player in the same way is very slim. Why? This narration comes mainly from the dynamic elements, only supported by static elements (to give the numbers context, so the chicken is chicken, not variable x).

In terms of loops, the most narratively important things played out on action-feedback and short-term cognitive loops. The whole drama that is important for me played out on this level: The desperate fight with the bandits, the putting out fires, the coop building, and the looming threat of starving in the winter. It was not preplanned by the team at Ludeon Studios. It came out from a multitude of small mechanics working together. In that space, I created my own plans and goals and played out my own dramatic stories, being as much an author of my own demise as the balance of the game. The game also has an overarching goal and end state that the player can reach to finish the game, but when you read my story and the stories of other players, this end goal rarely is brought up.

Now let me tell you a very different story, a story of grief but also hope and perseverance. This story, narration to be precise, happened in *Hellblade*, a third-person perspective action game that puts the player in the shoes of a troubled Pict woman on a mission to bring her lover from the dead.

The main goal is to descend to the lowest part of mythological hell, to bargain with Hella for the life of the main character, Senua's, dead lover. Senua even has a bag with his head attached to her belt, so there is a constant grim reminder of our purpose. While traveling, there are different obstacles to overcome. Environmental puzzles and quick, tense combat encounters. There is also a looming threat of a disaster, as Senua may fail, and this failure is much more painful for the player—if she dies too many times, the save file will be deleted, and the player will have to start their journey from the very beginning*.

* This is a high-stakes bargain on the side of the game and a way to align Senua's panic with players' emotions, so they also feel it. For many players, it worked like a charm, but others decided not to play the game, as they thought the game did not value their time. The trick is that there is no permadeath in this game. It is all a bluff.

Years have passed since I finished this game, but still, there are things that I remember vividly. Yet, those are not the puzzles, traversal and combat. It's Senua, her struggle, perseverance, and final acceptance of her loss. It was the moment when she was afraid and in despair, and my desire to take her to the end of her story. The narration in this game is very powerful and moving, yet the low-level mechanics, action-feedback loops, and short-term cognitive loops are not so important to its shape. The only thing that matters is getting to Hella, and bringing Senua's lover back*.

* There is one, very interesting element at the very end of the game, where a key aspect of narration is delivered by interacting with a short-term cognitive loop. When the final fight happens, the player cannot win, but they do not know that, so wave after wave of monsters they try to survive, yet the key to progressing the story further, is giving up.

I hope that the difference between how narration is created in those two examples is striking. Now, from this, we can try to strive for a form of generalization. A new lens that we can use when examining our game. As we know, everything is better when presented as a graph, so let's define our 2D space. On the X-axis, we state how much low-level

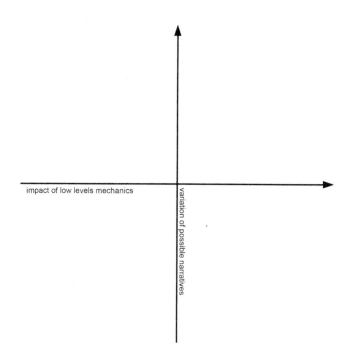

mechanics (the dynamic elements of shape) shape the overall narration, whereas on the Y-axis, we put how various possible narrations are.

Now, with this basic space, we can start to populate it with different games, to say where they lay. Of course, those axes represent a spectrum, but let's not fixate on the exact position of each game on it and rather conceptualize it as four quadrants.

In the lower left quadrant, we have games that have a low possible variation of narrations and a low impact of dynamic elements on this narration. *Uncharted* and *Hellblade* are good fits here. Especially in the first one, gameplay sections are just elements to move us from one narrative bit to another. Those elements are exciting, dynamic, and made extremely well, but their impact on the narration is small. We do not tell each other stories about Natan Drake, the guy who throws grenades and covers behind a barrel to shoot bad guys. *The Last of Us* series or the *God of War* series also lands in this space. All of those movie-like experiences land here.

In the upper left quadrant, we have games that have a high variation of possible narrations but a low impact of dynamic elements. This variation in narration comes from predefined nodes, big decisions that the player makes that put narration on a different track. As previously mentioned, *Life is Strange* lands here, but, to be frank, the variation in this game is not as high as in other representatives of this quadrant. Another example would be *The Witcher 3*—everyone who played it has a variation of this story, different choices, different quest outcomes, and different endings. Yet this variation does not come from dynamic elements. The narration does not care about our character builds or how we swing our sword—the key aspect is what we say in those predefined moments, what we will tell the Baron*. The narration of the witcher is an amalgamation of those choices. David Cage[1] games are also a clear pick here: movie-like experiences where the player pickles different options to move the

* The Baron story is one of the most recognized questlines in *The Witcher 3*. It tells the story of a man who lost his child, and depending on player choices, it may end in two very distinct ways.

story forward. Those are classic examples of a branching narrative. A tree-like structure in which players may pick different paths. So in this quadrant, we will have all of those *pick-your-own-adventure* types of experiences.

In the upper right quadrant, we have games that have a very high variety of possible narrations, and this variation comes from low-level mechanics. A crown example here is the *Dwarf Fortress*. A monstrosity of low-level simulation and procedural generation. The internet is full of stories of the absurd demise of dwarf colonies due to the elements of the simulation running underneath. None of those stories was prewritten, it's all the dynamic elements making their magic together. The previously mentioned *Rimworld* also lands here, the chicken story is an outcome of dynamic elements. All other anecdotes that players tell each other also come from them. All of those anecdote generators land here.

In the final lower right quadrant, we have games in which the variation of possible stories is not too high—all of them carry the

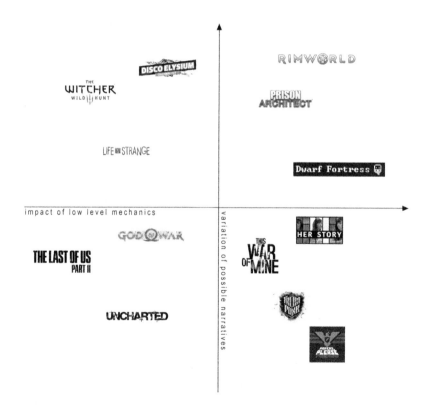

same message, but it comes out of those low-level mechanics. It gives them this unique flavor, a promise of deep co-authorship, yet, communicating more complex ideas. The game *Papers, Please*, is an example here. The narration about an oppressive, totalitarian state comes from small interactions and basic loops. Everything that the player does builds that image in their mind, yet still gives them enough freedom to shape the story in their own way. *Her Story* also lands here. In the end, all of us have quite a similar story in our heads about what has happened, yet how we got there is extremely personal. It reflects how we connect facts and what leads we go after. All of those mechanical stories will land in this quadrant.

So, now we populated our graph. Coming from that, we have four distinct categories:

- **Movie-like experiences**—games in which dynamic elements support the static elements, as the geist of the narration comes out of it. The narration from player to player is similar.
- **Pick your own adventures**—games in which dynamic elements support the static elements, as the geist of the narration comes out of it. The narration varies from player to player, but it comes from a predefined decision point (a branching structure of a narrative).
- **Anecdote generators**—games in which most of the narration comes from dynamic elements. The narration varies strongly from player to player and in each playthrough.
- **Mechanical stories**—games in which most of the narration comes from dynamic elements. Yet, the main geist of the narration is similar for all of the players but personalized.

All of those categories come with their own benefits, their own drawbacks, and pitfalls. Being conscious of where our game falls within those categories gives us information on what aspect we should look at and what problems we can anticipate. So let's go through those categories from that perspective.

Movie-like experiences are great for telling intricate, precisely directed stories. The control over the narrative is very precise, and gameplay does not interfere too much with what we want to tell. At least it shouldn't, it just should support the themes and character arcs. Yet it is not always the case, as this is the birthplace of the cursed ludonarrative dissonance*. The crown example of this is the story of a deer. The dramatic deer. It plays out in the new edition of *Tomb Raider* (2013), which depicts the origin story of Lara. She is young, inexperienced, and for the first time, put in a life-and-death situation. As so, the first time she needs to kill a deer is a heartbreaking moment. It is the first time she needs to take a life so that she can live one. It plays out in an emotional cutscene, where we see how moved she is by the act that she had to commit. Yet, ten minutes later, when the cutscene is over, Lara will nuke from the orbit the whole population of deers on the map without batting an eye, if only the player wishes so. There is no comment from her, no systemic response like those two characters are separate beings, not connected to one another—a ludonarrative dissonance. On the other hand, *The Last of Us 2* does this beautifully, the story about the cycle of violence and revenge plays out as clearly in cutscenes as it does in gameplay. Ludonarrative dissonance is averted.

> * Ludonarrative dissonance is a term coined by the designer Clint Hocking in a blog post back in 2007. It means a discrepancy between the narration of dynamic story elements and static story elements. Later writings move away from stating that this is something unique for games, and moves it more just to a tone mismatch between different parts of the narrative.

There is an interesting tension here, on one hand, the experience should be engaging gameplay-wise, and on the other, the narrative should be coherent. Checking on every step that gameplay does not work against the narrative is crucial. Especially since it is a *movie-like experience*, those static elements are the key, and everything else should support them—not the other way around.

There is also a second thing that comes from the fact that this is a *movie-like experience*. It has to compete for players' time with actual movies, as it uses a lot of the same toolbox to tell its story. This is where we come into budget impact. Especially in the current day and age, the player expects good actors, voice-overs, bombastic music scores, and amazing animations. All of that cost a lot of money. A lot. It is not a discouragement to not pursue this kind of game, but just a matter of being aware of what those games have to compete with if someone aims at mass market success. There are ways to do it smarter and cheaper, for example, *Hellblade* with their FMV elements, but still, it is not cheap. *Hellblade* had an alleged budget of 10 million dollars, and it was many years ago—now it is a lot more pricey.

Pick your own adventures are similar but have a slightly smaller expected quality (as in the player's mind is a lot more their story, not like in a movie). On the other hand, there is still a lot of high-quality content that has to be made that will never be seen by the player. An extreme version of that is *The Witcher 2*, where a choice in the middle of the game will lock the player in one of two possible second parts of the game. Yes, the whole second part. It is an extreme situation, but still, the case stands that branching narratives, outside mostly text-based games (*Disco Elysium*), blow up the budget quite significantly. How much it blows up depends on the type of branching. The *Witcher 2* example is one end of the spectrum, but on the other hand, games with a lot of small branches that are quickly resolved move us closer to the middle of the graph and can be an interesting way to give this adaptability without murdering the budget. As always, it is a balancing act.

Anegdote generators, on the other hand, are entirely different beasts. There are more like very complex sandboxes for the player to generate their own narration in. They also usually harvest the most powerful rendering engine in the world. Yes, I know, cliche, but still—the imagination! There are many reasons why that is the case. On the one hand, those games are created over very long periods. Meticulously adding new small systems that eventually create complex dynamics and stories. The two key representatives, *Dwarf Fortress* and *Rimworld* have been in development for the past 20 and 10 years, respectively, and they are still growing. Imagine the cost if we try to create them with less symbolic graphics. All of those little elements should have a representation, those distinct materials to create tools, those different social interactions between NPCs, those hundreds of procedurally generated monsters. Instead, in *Dwarf Fortress*, those things are represented by ASCII characters, and in *Rimworld*, by flat shapes with almost no animation. Yet, both of those games have huge market success and an extremely dedicated fan base, with thousands of hours invested in those games. The rudimentary graphics are not a problem, even more, they can be an asset—more is left for the player to imagine.

Due to the lack of a preplanned narrative, just broad strokes of what is the general idea, every playthrough is vastly different. Yes, most of them finish in disaster, but how the player gets there is unique and entertaining in their own way (my chicken story in *Rimworld*).

There is another side to that coin. One already mentioned thing is that those games take ages to create. Tweaking and creating all of those systems takes time and cannot be easily created in parallel, as this is a huge system of connected things. One step too quickly and every playthrough is a very similar snowball effect.

The second thing is that the control over narration is very limited. We can provide a structure for the playthrough. A tail of increasing odds and difficulties. *Rimworld* does it with a storyteller system that will scale the threats but also help the player if they are in a dire situation. *Dwarf Fortress* has similar mechanisms, like the relation between wealth and the frequency of attacks. Still, those tools provide a very rudimentary narrative structure. This is why I call them *anecdote generators*. It is not something bad, it is just a design choice, if we want to tell a coherent story exploring more complex topics, a strict emergent narration may not be the way. At least for now.

This brings us to a final category—*mechanical stories*. Those games tell stories mostly with dynamic elements supported by static elements, but the decision space is significantly smaller than in the case of *anecdote generators*. This gives an illusion of a very personalized narration for each playthrough, yet still, comparing those between players, we have a similar structure, arcs, narrative themes, and message.

The idea of that support between elements is a key here. System rhetorics* alone is not enough, as the first installment of *The Sims*, on a systemic level, is a critique of the consumerism

* More exploration of system rhetorics can be found in Chapter 5.

lifestyle. The more stuff we have, the more time we have to spend fixing and cleaning them, slowly but surely, removing a space for our Sim to live a life. But nothing else tells us in the game, so this story gets buried under everything else.

Dynamic and static elements give each other context, and in the case of those mechanical stories, it is most important. I find this path to be the most unique to tell a complex narrative to the player in a truly "gamey way." The power of co-authorship plays a huge role here, but still, we can communicate something more complex.

When I'm starting a new project, it is a conscious decision where I want to land on this graph. Every spot is as good as another, picking where depends on the type of game, budget, market share, target audience, and type of game. I usually work on narrative titles, so it makes sense to check the concept from this perspective, but of course, there are games when it is not needed (racing games, sports games, etc.).

If it were entirely up to me, I would stick as strongly as I can to the right side, as I think this is the unique and powerful way we can tell stories. It's also, in my opinion, a safer bet for indies, as the expected audio-visual fidelity of the project is different. Yet, when budgets are getting bigger, a lot bigger, games tend to move to the left. There is nothing wrong with that. The target audience gets proportionally bigger with bigger budgets (to break even), and this audio-visual fidelity starts to be very important, so there is less time and space to experiment. Yet, I hope that as some things are getting easier with new tools, we will have more big games moving to the right, exploring more strongly how we can speak in this unique voice of our medium.

Note

1 A game director working at Quantic Dreams, creator of, among many others, *Heavy Rain* and *Detroit: Become Human*.

7

PLAYING WITH AUTHORSHIP

ARTUR GANSZYNIEC

"Video games can never be art," Roger Ebert once said, and he was one of the most influential movie critics of his times, so he knew his arts. At the moment I'm writing this, almost two decades have passed since the words were said, and a lot of things changed, both in the world of film and video games, yet some of Ebert's arguments still ring, even if not true then at least intriguing. During his debate with Clive Baker, an author and video game writer, Ebert said that the interactivity of games is what makes it impossible to deliver a coherent artistic vision.

"One obvious difference between art and games is that you can win a game. It has rules, points, objectives, and an outcome." Ebert says. Movies and books are different. "Those are things you cannot win; you can only experience them." Would Shakespeare's *Romeo and Juliet* still be a masterpiece if the spectator could *win* a happy ending?

Jonathan Jones, an art critic publishing in the *Guardian* had similar doubts.

> (In a game) experience is created by the interaction between a player and a programme. The player cannot claim to impose a personal vision of life on the game, while the creator of the game has ceded that responsibility. No one 'owns' the game, so there is no artist, and therefore no work of art.

Case closed.

It's hard to argue that the player shapes how the game appears on the screen and that the influence is enormous. Even in the well-loved game about the jumping Italian plumber, where the story is very simple, it is the player who decides when Mario jumps; if he falls to

DOI: 10.1201/9781003325031-7

his death or succeeds, when; if he steps on a turtle, how many tries it would take to finish the level; and if the story would have an ending at all—there's always the possibility that the game becomes too hard to beat by that particular spectator.

What about the contemporary AAA Hollywood-style games about brave soldiers killing the enemy of the year? The games perfected the visual language of the film and the gameplay of "shoot to see the next part of the movie." The player has almost no influence on how the events develop, their role is to press the trigger or repeat a sequence of buttons to activate the next, carefully directed story-delivering sequence. Yet even in such games, when the player is in control, they decide where to look and when, when to run, and how long to explore the immediate surroundings. In other words, there are moments when the spectator is granted control over the camera and the direction of the protagonist. No movie would ever do that.

In open-world games, the designers have little or no control over whether a particular player sees the whole, rich world prepared for them. It is the player, who decides (sometimes unknowingly) in what sequence the secondary plots play out, or if they happen at all! If you handed such control over a book to the reader, every copy of *Moby Dick* would have a different amount of technical descriptions of the sailor's life, and some of the readers of *The Lord of the Rings* would never discover that Tom Bombadil even existed.

The situation gets even dicier when we look at cRPGs with branching stories, such as *Mass Effect* or *The Witcher* series. The player's choices determine not only which plots play out but also how the game ends and what the moral of the story is.

It seems reasonable to ask the question "how can you create art when your spectators interfere so much."

And yet, as any player or game developer can tell you, games can be art, and sometimes indeed are. Since 2004, BAFTA Game Awards have been honoring outstanding creative achievements in the video game industry. MoMA has an exhibition featuring games from *Pac-Man*, *Flower*, *Everything Is Going to Be OK*, to *This War of Mine*. The cooperation with the creators of *80 Days* prompted the British Library to research how to archive the works of interactive fiction. The aforementioned *This War of Mine*, 2014 wartime survival sim, has been added to the education ministry's official reading list for schools in Poland. The U.S. Supreme Court has ruled that video games are a form of expression entitled to First Amendment protection: "Like the protected books, plays, and movies that preceded them, video games communicate ideas—and even social messages—through many familiar literary devices ... and through features distinctive to the medium. That suffices to confer First Amendment protection."

Over the last few years, the way we write about games changed. After the release of *Cyberpunk 2077* the most interesting critique of the title concerned not the graphics, not the bugs, or the gameplay mechanisms, but the question, of whether a corporation infamous for its exploitative relationship with its employees has the moral right to produce a game in a genre focused on the critical examination of exploitative corporate practices. Journalists started treating games just like the other media, for better and worse.

I'd like to think that the critique is deeper because games themselves matured as a medium, and more and more developers aim not only at delivering a piece of entertainment but also at making a social commentary or creating an artistic statement of some kind.

Estonian hit *Disco Elysium* is a masterclass in noir mystery aesthetics, and at the same time, a deeply political game that allows you to challenge your preconception about fascism, communism, and the moral shortcomings of the centrist perspective. BAFTA winner *Unpacking* manages, with no words or characters, to paint a deeply personal, coming-of-age story about the search for one's identity. The innovative indie wonder *Before Your Eyes* you play by blinking, turns the player into the game controller and uses our basic physiological reactions to tell a story about dreams, death, and looking for the meaning of life.

Games move us, make us reflect, irritate and calm us, and comment on the world—they do everything that we expect from a mature medium. How could that be, if we have already established that the creators do not have full control over the final shape of their works?

It is possible to argue, of course, that all art is interactive; it is there in the very act of interpretation. Games are not unique in that respect. How many times have we gone back to a book or a movie that we once adored, only to find it boring, flat, or problematic? The way we see a work of culture is shaped by our experiences and beliefs and moderated by our level of focus and the emotional state we are in when reaching for a movie or a book. You cannot step in the same river twice and you cannot read the same book twice. You can write thousands of pages on that topic (looking at you Umberto Eco) and still only scratch the surface.

As authors, we have no idea what the spectators will think when confronted with our work. As spectators, we can interpret a work in many ways and we have no idea, no way to know, which of the interpretations was intended by the author if any. Yet, when we read a book, the pages are always in the same order, words do not jump from one paragraph to another, and the printed letters do not change. When we watch a movie, we always see the same scenes in the same sequence, and the actors say the same lines, in the same tone, in the same context. This is not the case when games are concerned. Every playthrough has the potential of delivering a different sequence of scenes, changing lines spoken by the characters or changing their context, exploring different plots, or at least changing the pace of the story. Neither books nor movies have that quality.

What about the novel *Hopscotch* by Cortázar, the one that you can read in two different sequences of chapters and get two different stories? When it comes to sharing control over how and what the content is presented, even simple games do more than the most interactive of books (just to be clear, I see choose-your-own-adventure type gamebooks as games). With books, as long as I stay focused and don't daydream instead of reading, I will see the whole text prepared for me by the author. With some games, even when I play fully focused, exploring every nook and cranny, I will see only a fraction of the content prepared by the developers.

In *The Witcher* series, whole scenes play differently and plots come to different conclusions, depending on the player's previous choices. In the interactive journalistic travel literature *Wanderlust: Travel Stories* every scene is described differently, based on the protagonist's current mood, which is constantly shaped by the player. When I play *Before Your Eyes*, my tears change what is displayed on the screen. But, what I find more important, I can be moved to tears by the game, despite the fact that—as the critics pointed out—the authors don't have control over their work.

So who is the author? Does a game even have an author? As a player and a game designer, I would argue that, yes every game has an author. Most games have two: the developer and the player. And both have firm control over their respective parts of the final work.

Games are very interactive, but the interactivity is defined and constrained by the developers. While playing *Mario*, I can decide if and when to step on a turtle, but I cannot stop and have a chat with it. In the Western-themed sandbox *Red Dead Redemption 2*, I can explore, at my own pace, the slice of the Old West that was prepared for me, but I cannot step outside its boundaries. During a dialogue in *The Witcher 3*, I can pick and choose between Geralt's reactions preconceived by the writers but I can't write my own response. Many games feel like you could do just anything, but this freedom of choice is, mostly, smoke and mirrors. As it often is with art, the spectator feels and sees more than is really shown.

As an author, I don't know which of the dialog options a player will choose, but I have full authorial control over how to construct the choice and what options to present. As a game designer, I have to think about my work differently as a movie director or someone writing a book, but that's nothing new. Opera and ballet also have their own specificities, and their own constraints imposed on their authors. Games are a specific medium and a specific craft, but they are not unique. Every author has to think about the medium they shape and plan how the intended audience will experience the work. As a game designer I must think about players interacting with the game, but—whatever Roger Ebert said—my relationship with the player is not a struggle over who's in control, but a conversation.

Let us focus on the message of the work of culture, on the moral of the story. As a rule, if a movie, book, or game moves us, it asks (directly or not) a question we can relate to. Then, over the course of the story, we have the occasion to observe various characters struggling with or trying to answer various aspects of said question, which leads to the outcome and moral planned by the author. But how can the author be sure that the story leads to the moral they planned, if the control over the course of the story is, to a bigger or smaller extent, in the hands of the player? Finding viable solutions to the problem is, at least in my opinion, the heart of the video game storytelling craft, and the solutions vary depending on the size and genre of the game.

On one end of the spectrum are games, where the author wants to retain full control over the moral of the story. In such cases, the beginning, the midpoint, the end and the main plot points will be the same for every player—probably carefully directed cutscenes. The player will have some control over how they overcome the obstacles in the protagonist's way, but the path the protagonist takes will probably be predetermined. The critically acclaimed game *The Last of Us 2* lets us experience in many, deeply personal, ways how violence breeds more violence, lets us use our smarts to survive in the deadly post-apocalyptic world, but gives us no control over how the fate of the protagonists will play out.

A mutant soap opera *Mutazione* gives us more control—although the main plot points are predetermined, and the game has one, directed ending, there are multiple middles we can shape as a player. All of them lead to the same, authored moral. Yet, the fact that we, players, can influence the outcome or sequence of particular scenes, lets us feel closer to the game and invest more emotions in the story. As a result, we read the predetermined, authored ending as something personal. We choose the path leading to the moral so we feel the moral as our own.

This is how the best open-world games operate. In the *GTA* or *Red Dead Redemption* series, we are led from one carefully directed in-game movie to another, from an intriguing opening through many thrilling twists to a moving and satisfactory finale. Yet, the heart of the game is the unrestricted sandbox play in between the movies, full of its own thrills, discoveries, and turns of fortune. Every playthrough is different, and every player experiences their own personal stories and system-generated anecdotes, yet the main plot and the morale of the story are the same for all.

Games with branching narratives such as the movie-like *Detroit: Become Human* or the more open-structured *The Witcher 3* give the player even more agency, and let them influence the course of action to a greater extent. The player's decisions shape not only the subplots and personal arcs of the NPCs, but also influence the main plot, pushing the story toward one of the predefined, and often dramatically different, endings. Yet, every one of the endings was carefully designed, scripted, and directed by the developers, who also made sure that the crucial plot points leading to a particular finale make sense and amount to a satisfactory story. In other words, if the authors want to give the players the ability to shape the narrative and choose their own ending, they have to prepare not only one story but a range of possible stories with their corresponding morals.

Preparing such an array of branching, consistent plots, and accommodating all possible combinations of the players' choices is far from trivial. Yet the difficulties—however significant—are mainly of a technical and production nature. From the authorial perspective, the task is as simple, or as hard, as always: to write a number of stories that make sense. When we look at the tasks like that, the authors still have all their usual tools at their disposal. There is a lot of craft in writing branching narratives, but from an artistic perspective, there is nothing unique about them. They still are authored stories, with directed endings and a predefined moral. The only difference is that the player decides, over a number of small choices, which of the endings will be played and what moral will sound out.

But what about games that are based not on a series of discrete choices made by the player, but on the interaction between the player and the game's systems? Can we grow art on the soil of thousands of optimization-focused microdecisions? Let's take a look at *Frostpunk*, a BAFTA-nominated city-building survival game, where we manage the last human settlement during a new Ice Age. As a player, we make two types of decisions: minute-to-minute economy-based choices necessary to run the city, and long-term decisions where we shape the laws and customs governing the daily life of the people in our settlement. The systems of the game are designed in such a way that the more draconian laws give better chances of survival than the more humane ones. How far every city slides toward totalitarianism depends on the sum of all decisions the player made, big and small. After the game ends, the player is explicitly shown what human cost was paid for the city's survival and is asked a question: Was it worth it? Every player has to find their own answer. The moral stays personal and, as such, it sounds louder and clearer, than it would if the answer was given to the player by the authors.

Even further on the spectrum, we will find games such as *Rimworld* or *Dwarf Fortress*, where the player manages whole simulated communities and ecosystems, and the level of complication and the number of systems allow anecdotes and mini-stories to appear that were not designed or even conceived by the authors. Situations emerge from the interaction between the systems and the player, with little or no control of the designers. Simulation-survival games ask very direct and basic questions about human nature, destiny, or the sense of life. The answers are deeply personal and sometimes equally deeply moving, but they stay personal, known only to the players who experienced them. The game and the designers are unable to see if and when they happened.

As authors of such games, we can only use systems, numbers, and text snippets to create a machine that asks the questions we want to ask, and helps the players generate possible answers—but we must accept that the results of the machine's work stay hidden from our eyes. Unless a player decides to share their playthrough on the Internet and comment on the moral they experienced.

Streaming services such as YouTube or Twitch allow us to see how different various playthroughs of the same game can be. This multitude of voices and shapes of the story, visible at first glance, is one of the arguments used by the supporters of the 'lack of authorial voice' take on games. But when we look at any one of the playthroughs as a separate work of culture, we can appreciate the results of the dialogue between the authors and the players. Seen from the outside games become performative art, where the designers set the stage on which the streamers perform for their audience.

No matter how big the audience is, whether the game is experienced by just one person, intimately immersed in the experience, or live-streamed and watched by thousands of spectators, the division of labor stays the same. The developers prepare a set of systems and pieces of content, possibilities, and constraints that constitute the whole space of possible playthroughs. The players create their own performances, using their decisions and interpretations to create a particular experience, built of layers of events, meanings, and emotions. Some of the performances can and, in my opinion, should be labeled as art.

What makes a particular performance of a game art? For the most part, it depends on how good at their craft the designers are because they decide how consistent the game's motifs and themes are, and how well the systems support the story and its moral. The player, on the other hand, decides the pacing, the minute-to-minute drama, and the emotions of the particular playthrough.

When we take a step back, we will see that the division of labor is not unique to games. After all, who is the "real" author of a movie, the director, the writer, the operator, the editor, the actors, the producer, or the VFX specialists? Who decides the success of a theater play, the director, the set designer, or the authors? What makes a piece of music great, the score or the performance? The distinction between the author-conceiver and the author-performer is as old as art itself, so probably as old as humanity. Games, which offer a more democratic division of authorship than let's say movies, play the same part in our culture as street theater, folk music, or stories told by the campfire, iterating the same grand design, but changing with every performance and every set of spectators.

Personally, I like to think about authorship in games, using a musical metaphor. I see the designers, programmers, and artists, as the composers working on the score, and I see the players as musicians, performing the piece before an audience. Every performance is based on the same sequences of musical notes, and yet every performance can use different instruments, arrange the score in a different way, imbue it with different emotions, and be delivered with different levels of mastery.

Every musical performance is different, and yet no one asks if music can be art.

8

WHY GAMES WILL ALWAYS BE POLITICAL

MARTA FIJAK

"Get this filthy political agenda out of my games," "It was a great game until they introduced politics into it," "Once you go woke, you go broke," "I hate this type of baiting on political issues." Who of us has not seen this kind of lovely discourse online each time a game does something as radical as introducing women* or more skin colors*? This cursed word, this filthy cancer that is slowly eating the soul out of games, this monstrosity—politics. Let's also be honest here—developers are as allergic to this word as players are. Ok, maybe not even developers, but the PR machine of many games is. *Battlefield 2042*[1] with its climate disaster is marketed as not political. *Modern Warfare*[2] with proxy wars and colonialism is not political. *Far Cry 5*[3] with the iconography of

> * Like when *Battlefield V* introduced women to the battlefield. Suddenly, the realism of World War II—expressed in this game mostly by 360 no scoping, and t-bagging—disappeared.

> * Like when *Animal Crossing* did it, but to be frank, the backlash back then was so weird that I'm pretty sure it was nothing more than trolling—still, the comment: "I hate this type of baiting on political issues." was about that situation.

racism is not political. *Division 2*[4] with its civil war is not political. Shockingly, even *Detroit: Become Human*[5] with strong apartheid undertones is seen as not political. Saying that your game is a political statement is seen as a gigantic nail to the coffin for many—this filthy, cursed word. But is making a game without politics, and broader, a worldview, even possible?

DOI: 10.1201/9781003325031-8

Before we dive into it, let's first define what "political" actually means and how often, when we say political, we usually mean a certain worldview. Laying on good practices of YouTube video essays, let's start with a Merriam-Webster dictionary, which defines politics as: "... *3a: political affairs or business; competition between competing interest groups or individuals for power and leadership (as in a government) ... 5a: the total complex of relations between people living in society; relations or conduct in a particular area of experience especially as seen or dealt with from a political point of view.*"

This quote is heavily edited, as most of it focuses on politics as "guiding or influencing governmental policy" and "winning and holding control over a government." Most of the games accused of being political are not about "that form of political"—the *Democracy* series, with its first release in 2005, is still going strong and is not boycotted or welcomed with backlash each time a new installment appears. To be honest, most of the games that are deemed by players political, like *Battlefield V*, are not political in terms of the whole definition. OK, not exactly, but players are not mad due to the "complex relations" between nations fighting in World War II or depictions of "competing interest groups or individuals for power and leadership." They are mad because of women. So we need to broaden our definition, and instead of talking about politics strictly, let's reframe this discussion and talk about worldviews in games.

Let's do the exercise again—what is a worldview? This is a broad concept, tackled by philosophy, religion, and dictionaries for centuries, but to simplify, we can define it as a set of stances on the following categories:

- Responsibility to others
- View of human nature
- Relationship of humans with nature
- Sources of ethical wisdom
- Equality with others
- Relationship between the individual and the state (That's politics!)
- View of the good life.

All of this seems to go into a bag with the label "political" on it. When *Battlefield 2042* says something about climate disasters, it is a statement about the relationship between humans and nature. When *Modern Warfare* says something about colonialism, it's a statement about equality with others and responsibility to others. *Far Cry 5*, *The Division 2*, and *Detroit: Become Human* follow the same suit. So I'm sorry to be the bearer of the bad news, but all of those games are "political" in this colloquial meaning, understood as having a specific worldview in them. The same applies to *Battlefield V* and *Animal Crossing*—full of "politics."

That's the thing, though, with humans creating games; it cannot be any other way. If you want to create a game without a worldview, you can't. You are a human*. If you want to do a game without a worldview, you would have to do it without humans

> * I hope so. Or not. You do you.

involved in the process. There is this lovely Polish saying, "Opinions are like butts. Everyone has one," and it is the same with worldviews. Yet, not every worldview is seen as political, and this is connected with how mainstream the given view is. Not every game is also read in this way, as depending on how "realistic" a given game is, we pay different attention to those messages*. No one is discussing the crushing of the little ones to

> * It's similar to the role of system rhetorics described in Chapter 5.

build a "bigger" future in *2048**

> * You know, that logic game where you merge numbers together to get higher numbers.

as a representation of oppression and exploitation. Later on, we will analyze how we can place different games on a graph* that tracks how mainstream a worldview is and how realistic a game is. Then, we

> * Everything is better as a graph.

will discuss how it impacts what we are doing, how we are leading teams, and how we communicate our game to the public.

Before that, though, let's stop for a moment and discuss why being aware of our inner worldview is important and why we should rely on it to make our games better. First of all, having an agenda in a game is not a bad thing, expressing our worldview is not a bad thing, and placing a certain political statement is not a bad thing. Why? Games are cultural goods. They are there to be consumed consciously. Games can be challenging, spark discussion, and communicate novel ideas. Frankly, I think they are better in the last one than any other medium because those ideas can be tested out in gameplay or experienced firsthand by the player. There is power in that. Yet, there is the other voice that says "But games are products" and so they should not be "offensive," just smooth out from controversy, so they can be digested by the maximum number of people. Yes, true, but also screw that. Not touching politics, not exploring things more controversial, unique, or unusual, gives us bland games*.

> * OK, there are other reasons for that, but for the sake of this chapter, let's focus on polishing out worldviews from games to make them so digestible.

Look at *The Last of Us 2*, which proudly waves its flag, stating opinions on many topics. I'm not even talking about LGBTQ+*, but rather human nature itself and the cycle of violence. Do I agree with its portrait of human nature? Oh no, and

> * We will get back to this, so put a pin in it.

this is great, as I can discuss this game in many different contexts. Not only me—the gaming and mainstream media did it, and probably your friends too. Yes, this part of the discourse was slightly covered by the eruption of anger from the "true fans" due to different reasons, but even with those controversies, this game sells faster than the first installment, reaching 10 million copies in two years. Am I saying this is solely because of its strong worldwide expression? Of course not, but I strongly believe that this is one of the reasons why this game is not bland. Because say what you want, this one definitely made some people choke, as they expected another smooth, digested, "non-offensive" product.

That's not the only example. Look at *Disco Elysium*, *This War of Mine*, or even *Cult of the Lamb*. I know that production is often about minimizing risks, but I feel that in many

> * I will explain later. For now, please believe me that a poo-collecting sheep has to do anything with the discussed topic.

places, we overcorrect so strongly that we rip a huge part of the possible experience by removing the human worldview from it. What's left is hollow in a way. Of course, as mentioned before, not all games are like that. *Rocket League* and *Tetris* are not hollow in that sense. Their focus is on a different thing. Yet when we want to construct a more complex narrative, this edge removal, in my opinion, is a reason for a bland experience.

Outside of games having the possibility to be a statement or not being bland, there is also a marketing edge to all of it. Most of us are in this reality to where make more games, we need to sell the previous one. Even outside of economic incentives, we want our games to be played. So the first step is to draw the player in. This unique worldview can be a thing that makes you different in an oversaturated market. It can give a nice conversation starter, piquing interest by tackling something that no one is talking about. Yet, it is a double-edged sword, as it may also alienate the possible players—as usual, it highly depends on the situation. This audience alienation is also not only a marketing concern. Not all games are made for profit. Sometimes there is a message we want to spread, an experience we want to show, or things that we think will make the world a better place. Yet, saying it upfront may be counterproductive. It will lure in people who already agree with you or, if you are lucky, people who are on the fence on a given subject. You may want to reach further, to people from the other side of the worldview spectrum to build understanding and dialogue and not preach to the choir. In those situations, making your worldview not a main selling point may be a wise approach. *A Normal Lost Phone* (2017) released by Accidental Queens does something like that. It markets itself as a puzzle/adventure game about uncovering the truth about, you guessed, a normal lost phone. With this simple premise, according to creators, this game was able to change some players' views of LGBTQ+ issues. Those people would pick this game if they knew what it was about, but they thought it was just another lost phone.

There is also a creative liberation part to all of that. Over-sanitizing our games creates overcorrection. Those inoffensive smooth jellos of an experience that go down in one gulp. Yet, when we embrace different worldviews in games, we can push them further. We can explore even things outside our comfort zone, things that are not our worldview but may be fun in a playful setting*, we can ask ourselves questions like "What if?" and we can ask those questions to the players. Exploring those in games, especially systemic ones, can be a fresh and interesting ride, showing emergent behaviors that we never thought

* Think creating and leading a cult in the *Cult of the Lamb*—if it were a hyper realistic game, this would be very awkward, so to say.

about. For example, I would love to play a hardcore libertarian city builder. Especially since it is as far from my personal values as it can be, but it sounds challenging and interesting. I would like to play a modern-day RPG in a world where the main source of ethical wisdom is the *Warhammer 40k* rule book. Frankly, I wouldn't mind starting a cult. There is a fine line here, though. Those what-if questions, those explorations, can quickly turn into something distasteful and with strong edgelord-like quality.

Let's try to find where this line lies, and what better way to do it than with a graph*! Of course, as in previous chapters, this is not a proper "scientific" graph. It is rather a conceptual framework when thinking about worldviews in our games. It is a kind of simple

* I strongly believe that literally every problem can be solved with a graph.

compass that, on the one hand, should push away from being bland, but on the other hand, should steer clear of edge lord territory. It's also a simplification. It does not consider every aspect of a game and only focuses on selected dimensions. Those dimensions are:

- **Worldview-o-meter**—How common is the given worldview in our target audience demographic? Is this the status quo? Is this our current mainstream reality? Or is this some very out-there idea that we are servants to trees?*

* Due to the nature of our medium, games for only domestic markets are not a big thing. Games are international products (Chapter 3), and at this scale, I look at an averaged-out English-speaking player.

- **The vibe of realism**—How realistic is the setting? The graphic?

The time period, etc.? How much mental gymnastics does it require to imagine it as part of our current reality?

By drawing out those two axes, we get something that looks more or less like this:

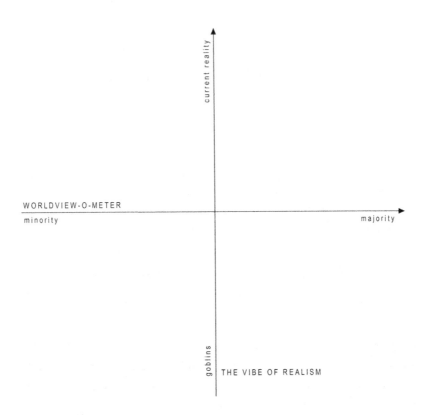

Now we have a 2D space on which we can start to place some games. On the far right, we will have titles such as the *FIFA* series, *Assassin's Creed*, etc.—the safe, edgeless mass-market things. To be clear, those games are good in some of their aspects, engaging, well made, etc., but in terms of interesting world-views, challenging, or sparking discussion, this is the land of the bland. What's fun is that if we move slightly (slightly!) to the left, we will go to those awful "political games"—people of different genders, colors, and sexual orientations in games.

Taking into account the start of this chapter, nothing further to the left should exist, as we already know that games are not political, and if they become political, they spontaneously combust and cease to exist. Eh, such a waste of a very nice graph space …

So, what's there on the left? A lot of things! We have *Spec Ops: The Line*, *This War of Mine*, *The Last of Us 2*, *Bioshock*, *Papers Please*, *Disco Elysium*, *Cult of the Lamb*, etc. There's even more! There are games like *Hatred* or *Postal*. All of them are placed in different parts of the graph, tackling delicate matters (*This War of Mine*), questioning the status quo narrative of their time (*Spec Ops: The Line*), playing with unusual ideas (*Cult of the Lamb*), or exploring dubious moral stances (*Hatred*). Some of them are even almost a political manifesto—I'm looking at you, *Disco Elysium*!

When we put them on the graph, it starts to look more or less like this:

Of course, I have an agenda representing it like that, as I see a sweet spot in there. A good space between being too edgy and alienating audiences and, on the other hand, being bland and unchallenging with the things we explore. Imagine *This War of Mine*, the same gameplay, but not about humans in a city strongly resembling Sarajevo during the siege, but a fantasy land full of humanoid critters. The system rhetorics would still be the same, but would the game be such a discussion piece? On the other hand, try to imagine the *Cult of the Lamb*, but not with lambs, but with humans. With realistic graphics. Yes, a cult simulator where you can feed poop to your fellow cultists. It would put this game on the fringe of discussion as an edgy nightmare. A *Binding of Issac* is another game that would not survive such transformation—especially since even in its current form it is distasteful for many*.

* I write these words while having a *Binding of Issac* hat on my head. I love that hat.

There is a fine line when exploring different worldviews in the media. Of course, sticking to this sweet spot of "interesting and not off-putting" is a matter of artistic intent. Nothing is stopping us from going all into the land of *Hatred*. Just one thing on that note, especially since it also came up during the promotion of *Cyberpunk 2077*. To be precise, there was a media storm about one of the in-game posters, as it over-sexualized transgender characters. The defense was that it was a condemnation of this type of stereotypical approach. Showing something is not the same as stating an opinion about it. Usually, showing something without a comment is a form of endorsement of it. Putting it in context, showing consequences, having characters react to it, etc. are a commentary, but just showing these are not.

Getting back to the graph, though, it seems that there is a relation between how far we can go and how realistic we are to still be palatable to the general public. Drawn on the graph, it looks more or less like this:

On the far right, we have the land of the bland. Just remember, if your game is there, it does not mean that it is bad. Its focus should be elsewhere, that's all. On the far left, we have the edge lord's land. Those games of questionable taste are built on controversy. They are as far from the acceptable discourse as we can imagine. Then, we have the border territories. Everything above the sweet spot land may be too much to stomach for the general public. Everything below is going again into the land of bland and does not have much potential to be conversational peace. The sweet spot is this strip of the graph in between. Games that are not afraid to tackle, show, or discuss worldviews that are not perfectly aligned with the mainstream. Yet, depending on how far other they are, they balance it out with how realistic they are. This is the land that I think we should strive for, not being afraid of weird worldviews, bold statements, and politics. The medium is mature enough to tackle every subject, so let's also dismantle this curse of politics in games, and embrace it instead.

That should be the closing statement of this chapter, yet, as you can see, it is not. There is a tension here—tensions between treating games as a means of expression and communication but also as a commodity. I switch back and forth between talking about putting bold statements in games and exploring controversial topics, but at the same time not alienating the audience. Not any audience, but the mass market™. This undefined mass of potential consumers we can convert into players. I talk about drawing them in by expressing less typical worldviews, both as an endorsement to have a more pluralistic discussion inside of games but also as a marketing edge that may be a unique selling point. Cynicism mixes with sincerity. This is a tension I don't know how to resolve. It's a tension that, I think, every creator has in the modern day and age. So I put this chapter down on paper, hoping for more mature and diverse games in the future, but I disguise it as a marketing strategy. Or maybe it is the other way around?

Notes

1 https://www.ign.com/articles/battlefield-2042-climate-change-social-commentary-gameplay-reasons-political
2 https://www.vg247.com/modern-warfare-not-political
3 https://www.polygon.com/2017/12/15/16778928/far-cry-5-politics-religion
4 https://www.polygon.com/e3/2018/6/12/17451688/the-division-2-is-not-making-any-political-statements
5 https://kotaku.com/despite-political-overtones-david-cage-says-detroit-is-1795939952

9

AUTHOR AS A GROUP ENTITY

How It Feels to Be One of 500 Voices

MARTA FIJAK

Death Stranding, a game by Hideo Kojima, was made by around 80 people.[1] *American McGee's Alice* was made by around 90 people.[2] Sid Meier's *SimGolf** was done by around 106 people.[3] Yet, *Getting Over It with Bennett Foddy* seems to have been done

> * I know it looks weird but it's a great game. Trust me.

almost in its entirety by Bennett Foddy,[4] but I hope that you get the point*. Those team sizes are also rookie numbers. *Red Dead Redemption 2* has more than 4000 people in the credits,[5] and *Cyberpunk 2077* is just slightly less—around 3.5k.[6]

> * The point being that there is a single name on the box and dozens of people behind it.

Who is the author of those games? The capital A author, the Auteur, the creative force behind it. Is this the whole blob of people in the credits? The whole company? The person whose name is on the box? Who is to blame when things take a turn for the worse, and who is to praise when they go great?

Authorship in itself is not a solid concept. It's a culturally constructed category, deeply ideological and strongly connected to issues with distributions of power. Defining authorship is a monstrous task that has already claimed many smarter victims than me. Foucault approached it from the perspective of "production." Stefano Gualeni came from the game studies angle. Barthes said that the author is dead. There is also a question: Do games even have authors? Most big games are made for money. They are products and need to

DOI: 10.1201/9781003325031-9

be sold. Does a yogurt, a hammer, or a wheelbarrow have an author? Sure, it was made by someone, but is there a capital A author behind it in the modern age of mass production and automatization? Games are not the same as a hammer, but as I write it, and when you read it, hundreds of people work on games that have one reason to exist—there is some kind of profitable IP lying around, and it would be great to milk it further. Is it so much different from a new toothpaste being developed because someone saw a new possible marketing angle in a bizarre tik-tok trend about tooth color?

Authorship in our modern day and age is a messy concept, and it affects not only games. Let's look at serious things*—modern art. It can be a multidisciplinary effort, just like game dev. Even if a big-scale installation is credited

* As serious as autonomous grand pianos not killing museum visitors can be.

to one person, rarely is it entirely done by them. There is a group of collaborators, engineers, and technicians that work on such constructions. Let's take, for example, Offroad, an installation by Céleste Boursier-Mougenot. It's a rather sizable piece of art that consists of three full-scale grand pianos autonomously roaming in the exposition space. I haven't seen this in person, but it seems that those are non-aggressive, gentle creatures that try not to ram into each other and also have visitor safety in mind. This installation is an achievement of many, from various backgrounds and specializations—mechanical engineers, programmers, and probably even piano tuners (even if gentle and autonomous, those are still musical instruments). Yet, the author of this work is Céleste Boursier-Mougenot. It makes sense in the world of modern art. Yes, probably Mr Céleste called all of the shots and made the important decisions, but there is also a more prosaic aspect to that. Anne Sauvageot quoted: "A work of art is legitimised by being assigned to an author, and the art market does not really favour the plural … ." This diagnosis is as unexpected as the ending of any Scooby Doo episode—under the ghost costume, the market forces are hidden. More broadly, the market—both the financial one and the market of esteem and pride. The author is a brand in themselves, and with the commodification of not only art but also our identities as authors, a single name is a lot "easier" to sell.

Yet, it would be a hasty conclusion to say that the problem with authorship is an issue of our modern, highly technological society.

Let's take Peter Paul Rubens's paintings* as an example. Many of them are not "pure Rubens," so to speak. At some point in his life, he led an artist

* As serious as baroque paintings can be—a lot of "selfies" and bombastic and religious extravaganzas.

workshop with many more people involved in a single painting. Sometimes he did just the key elements (faces, hands, etc.); sometimes, he did an oil sketch and then left the finishing of the work to his pupils; and sometimes he did the whole thing himself. Still, all of those paintings are Rubens's paintings, almost like Hideo Kojima games.

This brings us back to the question of authorship in games—who is the author, who is a contributor, and who and how gets mentioned in the credits? Due to the multidisciplinary character of games, we probably look at this aspect as a multidimensional construction*. The answer to the question of who the author is depends on which aspect we are focusing on. As previously

* Yet, on the other hand, past and modern art is also multidisciplinary. It seems to be the property of such cultural and ideological concepts.

mentioned, Stefano Gualeni proposes to look at the question of authorship from the perspective of "how" and "what." The author is not the person who answers the first question (engineers, technical designers, QA, producers, etc.) but the second one, so the designers, game directors, writers, etc. People who decide the content of the game. It may be a useful approach when analyzing games from the perspective of game studies, looking at games as a cultural expression, but it seems too reductive from the perspective of game development. The act of being an author/co-author of a game has real-life ramifications for the developers involved. That's why being removed from the credits is sometimes used as a punishment for leaving the company or just a way to divide people who make games into different categories—some get the prestige of being credited, and some don't.[7] There can also be an inverted situation where people who worked on the game don't want to be credited*. This aspect of attributed

* Sometimes, due to the overall quality of the product and sometimes as an escalation of interpersonal conflicts.

authorship impacts our ability to make a living by doing what we love. When looking for your next job, games on which you are credited are a strong bargaining chip*. The aspect of creative freedom* is also one of the things that draw people to this industry—the ability to express ourselves in a medium that we love. When going through the job offers, many of them list a high degree of ownership and options to really affect the shape of things as key pluses of a given position*.

* Lately this seems to change with the length of big-budget projects and the number of cancellations. It seems that experience alone, even without a release, is seen as valuable enough.

* Within the boundaries of the vision for the given project.

* Just after Fruit Fridays and "competitive salary" without stating what the ranges are.

Guillermo Del Toro, in the movie about Hideo Kojima: *Connecting Worlds,* states that "*... only the person in charge of the orchestra is the author.*" It reduces the group of people to contributors and the author—I have a lot of mixed feelings about this quote. On the one hand, it's reductive and can be harmful. On the other hand, Hideo Kojima seems to be a very special case, similar to Wes Anderson. From very far away, without even seeing it clearly, you know who made this particular work of culture. Yet, games are millions of micro-decisions that shape the whole experience. Those micro (and macro) decisions also affect other people in the team. Inspire them, change their decisions, etc. Those inspirations are not one-way streets. It's not only The Big Decision Makers (game directors), who inspire people below them, but it also works the other way around. Especially, as every game goes through that early exciting stage of ideas explosions, but then as the production progresses, a process of pruning starts. Paraphrasing Jenova Chen, the game is finished when the last unneeded element gets removed*. Maybe the one that cuts is the author? The one

* I cannot find the interview I took it from, so let us hope Mr. Chen is not mad about this attribution. Also, never mind the source, I still stand behind this thesis.

who leaves only the core of the product*? Sometimes those decisions are made by producers or even business development people (more about it later). Are all of them authors? Is one of them the author?

> * I'm in pain every time I write that a game is a product, but on the other hand, I find this cold and sobering perspective important.

We can probably agree that games are collaborative efforts created by many people—so maybe saying that they are co-authored by everyone involved is justified. Merriam-Webster dictionary states that an author is "one that originates or creates something." So everyone in development has a thing that they authored and can pinpoint, and the whole game is a collaborative effort of many authors. Case solved, Merriam-Webster to the rescue—essay over. Or is it? What about producers? Testers? Marketing? Business development? And what about the outsourcing? Are they authors of the game or only of some assets? It seems that this approach, exactly the same as Guillermo del Toro's approach, is reductive and does not grab the modern multifaceted authorship, where the creation is an outcome of authorial intent, collaborative work, technical skills, and market pressure. Yes, I like the notion of everyone being co-authors of a given game. Yet, I think forcing someone to be a co-author of a game can be as unfair as taking away their right to call themself co-author.

Over the years, I've been quite often involved in the recruitment process, going through hundreds of CVs. Mind you, those were also high-level positions, leads, directors, etc., and as my memory serves me*, 95% of CVs did not have a list of games that the given person was a co-author or an author.

> * Take it with a grain of salt. My memory may not be too good, as most of it is just bizarre Japanese games.

Yet most of them had a list of games that a person has worked on. Not an attribution to creation but a marker of a labor exchange. Of course, this is not "data." This is an anecdote. Yet this feeling prevails when I talk to my colleagues at events, 95% of them do not talk in terms of being a creator or an author. A contributor at most. They performed a service in exchange for compensation. Yes, they are proud of the things they worked on, but they are not the authors of the thing usually. Even when we discuss some specific aspect of the game, like a given implementation of snow melting, or an innovative inventory system, people tend to say they "worked on it."

When Polish journalists write about someone that "they are a co-author of *The Witcher* game," it's usually met with a smirk in the industry. It's seen as a marketing stunt and a "clickbaity" approach to the topic. Almost like it is in bad taste to appropriate authorship*. It seems weird in the modern day of personal brand and solo achievements. If I had to pinpoint the reason for this phenomenon, I would probably turn toward the intimate understanding of the game development process that developers have. How much of a collaborative effort the whole thing is. The game is the brainchild of the whole team, from the QA intern to the producers and ending on the audio director. The impact of each of these people varies, but still, everyone left their own unique fingerprint in a way. Of course, each of those elements is, at the end of the day, guided by the project's vision. Yet, the same project vision developed by two different teams would be an entirely different game at the end of the day. I'm ready to bet my money that if we took the same vision and the same top management (directors and leads) and gave them two different but equally skilled teams, the games would be like night and day*. So all of those people are co-authors. Of course, we can try to explore this intellectual construction further, turning it into a wired mutation of the Theseus Ship debacle*.

* It may be the very specific bubble I exist in, one of modesty and insecurity. Maybe it's a European approach? It would be cool to have a more extensive study on this topic.

* Sadly, I cannot prove this thesis with an experiment, as time travel has not been invented yet at the time of writing this book. Also, there is the case of Hideo Kojima, the only person with whom I'm not so sure. An exception proving the rule?

* The debacle goes as follows: We have a ship, Theseus's ship. It stands there and rots over time. So, to keep it in good shape, we remove broken elements, and replace them with new identical ones. The question is: At what step of this process, the ship stops being Theseus's ship?

How many developers should we switch so that the player would see the game as a significantly different project? Getting back on track, though, it seems that it's rather natural that everyone involved in the development is a co-author.

Maybe there is a different reason for game developers' modesty. Co-authorship also comes with responsibility. I'm a co-author, so I take responsibility for what I give to the players. I'm responsible for the quality, the content, the message, and the overall experience in the end. Is this responsibility fair when games are made by teams of more than 80 people? The probability that the moral standing, worldview, and artistic sensitivity of all of those people overlap enough is slim. Indeed, some companies check some of those things during the recruitment process. While working at 11 bit studios, a question that I once heard and then asked many times was: "What are some elements of culture that had the biggest impact on you?" It was a way to spot some kind of cultural capital and maturity. Is this a perfect tool? Absolutely not, but it gives a "vibe"*. Yet as far as I know, it was used mostly in designer recruitment, and I don't know if it is still

* The answer to this question was only a small element of an overall evaluation.

used. There is a moment in production, a certain pressure when you need a person with the right skills. Now. The fact of a different "vibe" loses importance. Personally, while recruiting designers, I skipped this question a few times due to those reasons. When this "vibe" is misaligned, people can fundamentally not agree with the game's content. It's easier to say you worked on it, but you are not a co-author. Still, games can be art, yes, but game development is also a job, and picking a project that you personally stand 100% behind is a rare privilege that only a few of us can have.

Oh, and let's not forget the Internet™. You know which Internet I'm talking about—the angry Twitter mob type*. People disguised as cartoon avatars can get very pissed about many

* Dying slightly at this moment due to the dying of Twitter itself. Sorry, X.

different things. Then, anyone who in their mind is an author becomes a target. Harassment, stalking, swatting, death threats, and every other disgusting tactic that people use to show they don't agree with something. Being a contributor or person who "worked on" something seems slightly safer in this setup than standing proud and saying that they are one of the co-authors. Especially when they had no say in the matter that the Internet™ is currently pissed about.

In a perfect world, we all would be co-authors on an equal creator footing, joining like-minded people because we agree on what kind of experience we want to offer the players*. Indeed, some people would have more decision power, some less, but everything would be discussed and backed up by arguments. Starting from the vision of the game, the first moment when things get heated—as things in a creative process tend to get—we would have a sacred document, which would be used as the final say. There are a lot of questions

> * My perfect world; yours may be vastly different. For all I know, your perfect world may be a *Mad Max* dystopia where we eat each other— you do you. In that case, yes, I'm judging you, and I would also like to ask you if everything is alright.

about that kind of a perfect world, for example, scalability* or discussion overhead, but allow a girl to dream. Yet we do not live in a perfect world. In many instances, the co-authors don't have a lot to say

> * Another thing is the question of "why scale up" and if this is a dead end—more about it is given in Chapter 4.

about the fundamental "what kind of experience do we want to offer the players?" because, once again, there is this Scooby Doo villain—the demand of the market.

If you ever worked on a big-scale product, you know the beginning of the process. The marketing analysis, the definition of the target demographic, the possible value of a given product through the lens of features, the minimal and expected return on investment (ROI), and the budget. All of those things shape the initial pitch, and the bigger the budget, the bigger the risk aversion. Big games are here to make big money. Especially now when the biggest games have a budget of more than 200 million dollars.[8] It's hard to convince anyone to fund a very ambitious and niche concept on that scale, as we are discussing a product that has its target demographic and an expected return. Especially when we talk about publicly traded companies, as those do not answer to players directly. A happy player is a means to get to the real person you have to make happy—the investors, as when you enter that space, you promise infinite growth to your stakeholders. Can we even talk about authorship in such a situation, where artistic purpose is just a tool to get a line graph to go up? Let's not be naive, though. The fact that big games are made for big money does not mean there are no other reasons for their existence. It's a multidimensional spaghetti of motivations, social constructs, ROIs, human needs, and social capital. In this wet spaghetti of indefinable things, we need to find ourselves as authors, creators of marketable goods, and workers.

Finally, maybe this is a game of accumulating social capital and creative power. Proving game after game that the ROIs are ok, and you, as a single person, can lead the creation of something remarkable. This way, one day, someone will look on the market and, against all "trends," give you money, so you can make a big budget game about walking*, and then you can be its sole creator, the author, or at least the only author that matters.

* I'm a big fan of the design of this game and the bravery of investing in this pitch.

Notes

1 https://www.videogameschronicle.com/news/hideo-kojima-claims-he-was-involved-in-15-disciplines-for-death-stranding/

2 https://www.mobygames.com/game/2703/american-mcgees-alice/credits/windows/

3 https://www.mobygames.com/game/5700/sid-meiers-simgolf/credits/windows/

4 https://www.mobygames.com/game/99109/getting-over-it-with-bennett-foddy/credits/windows/

5 https://www.mobygames.com/game/115902/red-dead-redemption-ii/credits/playstation-4/

6 https://www.mobygames.com/game/128136/cyberpunk-2077/credits/windows/

7 https://www.washingtonpost.com/video-games/2021/05/18/video-game-credits-policy/

8 https://www.ign.com/articles/the-last-of-us-2-and-horizon-forbidden-wests-budgets-revealed-ftc-documents

10

SLOW GAMES

ARTUR GANSZYNIEC

Let me tell you a very personal story. It is a story about an idea, its conception, its contact with reality, and the inevitable changes that follow. I cannot tell you how the story ends because it is a constant work in progress—but I will tell you about the journey.

The story started a few years ago when I turned 40—a perfect moment to indulge in self-reflection. At that moment in my life, I was overworked (a burden that I personally put on myself), I was balancing on the edge of burnout (looking back, on the wrong side of the edge), and I started having some health issues—all in all, I decided that I had to slow down. And when I did, I noticed that my taste in games and my needs as a player changed. I was not sure if the change was caused by my mental state, or if my mental state helped me to notice the change in my preferences. Never mind the cause, I realized that I needed a slower pace not only in life but also in my entertainment. I needed games that would slow down with me.

The problem was that most games I played at the time—and, as far as I could tell, also the most games on the market—operated on strong, adrenaline-fueled emotions: anger, fear, frustration, and euphoria. And I had more than enough of those feelings in my real life. I started to look for games that would operate on curiosity, hope, warm satisfaction, and coziness; games that would feel relevant to my adult life. I didn't want my games to scare me and excite me, I needed a space to reflect and grow at my own pace. I didn't find many such games but those I found moved me deeply.

I shared my thoughts with friends and colleagues and noticed that I was not alone in the longing for slowness, and realized that the need for slowing down was quite an old one. In other words, I was reminded of the slow movement. The movement started in Italy in

 DOI: 10.1201/9781003325031-10

the 1980s, with the first Slow Food restaurant—which was established as a reaction to a known fast food chain entering the country. The food the slow restaurant served was sustainable, local, organic, and wholesome. The idea took off, and soon we could witness the emergence of slow architecture, slow fashion, the philosophy of slow living, etc. I took a dive into the history of the movement and emerged with an idea. We needed slow games.

I searched the Internet and because, at that time, I found nothing that I resonated with, I decided to write down my thoughts and share them with the world.

Let me quote the manifesto, as it was written in 2019.

Slow Gaming Manifesto

I believe that games are a medium for telling stories and employing specific tools, but they are not inherently more or less effective than other media. I believe that this medium is capable of telling the whole range of human stories, not only those about conflict, overcoming frustration, and gaining mastery of a skill. I believe that the creator-player co-authorship is unique for games as a medium.

- I want games that treat me as an adult, someone capable of thinking, feeling, and understanding.
- I want games that connect with me not as toys but as tales of common human experience.
- I want games that challenge not my skills and reflexes but my assumptions and feelings.
- I want games that encourage me to take a break and come back later.
- I want games that let me experience them at my own pace.
- I want games that give me space to grow.
- I want games that are slow.

Why Do We Need a Label?

There are a number of games that fit the criteria but they are hard to find. I hope that establishing a tag, a label, will make it easier to talk about games in terms of the values they represent; and to create a space where we can gather, discuss, present ideas, exchange experiences, and share our work.

Drawing inspiration from such movements as slow living or slow food is intentional, as I think that slow gaming could be more than a collection of products sharing similar characteristics, and become a philosophy of game design and production.

Slow Games Philosophy

This part of the post is more of an optimistic hypothesis than a tested set of business practices—at the moment I think these could be the pillars of a slow gaming studio.

- **Sustainable development**: It is focused on the long-term existence of the studio, not on short-term growth and profit maximization, in a way that is not damaging to the lives and creativity of the team.
- **Local inspirations**: It is focused on games made by actual people, based on their personal experiences, grounded in their own relations to other people, and focused on ideas and things that are close to the team (emotionally when not geographically).
- **Originality of voice**: It is the form of the game reflecting the shape of the story, not trends of the market, authenticity of the message, exploring new themes, especially those deemed as not suited for games.
- **Wholesomeness**: Not exploiting fears but encouraging growth, not manipulating but being open and honest, having faith in a player's ability to understand the message and add to it, making games enriching both the player and the creators.

I would love to hear your thoughts, to discuss and share ideas. But I will also be happy if you read the post and think about it for a while.

Take your time.

Other Takes on Slow Games

It may come to you as no surprise that I found no other interesting mentions of slow games due to my inferior Google-fu, not due to the fact that there weren't any. Sometime after I published the manifesto and got some traction, two other takes were recommended to me.

The first one was titled *Slow Games Movement Manifesto*,[1] and in contrast to prior attempts to tackle the topic, I didn't focus on how to play or review games (at least not solely), but on how to make games.

This manifesto caught my eye with a quote that—at least in my opinion—cut straight to the chase: "The vehicle of video games is careening out of control, and we're constantly trying to hand over the reins to people we believe are more in-control. The **slow games movement** asks if it's not a better idea to try to just slow … down."

The text tackled the idea of slow design and how it connected to technological progress and forced obsolescence of game development tools. It discussed slow engagement and curation, the ways games existed in our culture, how long they were perceived as relevant, and how we could change our engagement patterns to make more space for reflection.

What piqued my interest the most was the take on slow management and the yearning for a slower industry. The text was deliciously non-conforming and political (in a way that I learned to appreciate) and proposed systemic changes to counteract what were mostly systemic problems. It spoke of flexible working hours, the need to improve wages, unionization, and using the old "your dream job in the games industry!" excuse for poor working conditions.

The manifesto ended on a jarring, sobering note: "It could be said of any of the ideas of this manifesto that they are difficult (if not impossible) to manifest … . This is true."

I resonated deeply with the need to slow down, with the questions about why we engage with games as players, and what goals could we set for ourselves as designers. Most of all, I resonated with the need for a slower, more nurturing work environment.

Much later, I stumbled upon a report from The Twelfth Annual Game Design Think Tank, Project Horseshoe 2017, summing up a workshop called *Coziness in Games: An Exploration of Safety, Softness, and Satisfied Needs*.[2] Technically speaking, the phrase "slow games" was not mentioned in the text but the discussed questions and ideas were almost perfectly aligned with the slow gaming movement explorations.

The text saw *coziness* as an ingredient that could be applied to a wide variety of game genres, a characteristic growing from abundance, safety, and softness. Adding coziness, the text argued, would produce games focused on the higher tiers of Maslow's hierarchy of needs: On connectedness, self-reflection, and mastery. Just what I needed—I thought.

The report discussed many ideas that I touched upon in my manifesto and proposed deliberate design tools for adding coziness to games, such as intrinsic rewards and ways of achieving cozy aesthetics. It analyzed how games created cozy emotions and how such emotions affected players and game communities. It noted how playing on fight or flight response, competition, using extrinsic rewards, and zero-sum economy played on basic needs and destroyed coziness.

There were in-depth discussions of cozy ambient narratives, cozy story archetypes, and designing cozy relationships with NPCs. I was stunned by the depth of the analysis and wholeheartedly recommend reading the report in full.

But it was the last paragraphs that got me thinking again. The designers taking part in the workshop discussed coziness as a development practice and as a radical philosophy for making games. The phrase "crunch is not cozy" became one of my favorite quotes.

The text ended with an invitation to radically cozy game-making, which I want to quote if full:

> Dear designer whom I care for, I wish for you that game-making be a refuge from the storm. I take joy from the games you make, and I hope you feel fulfilled when you make them. As a colleague, I want you to feel safe to express your inner self, to take creative risks in your craft. As a friend, I wish that you can escape the ever-present hurry and pressure of our industry and world, into a restful, healthy practice. If you feel comfortable, I invite you to make a game that reflects those moments in your life that were meaningful, where you were content and cared for. I invite you to make a game that offers moments for players to reflect and be at ease. You don't have to show it to me; you don't have to share it with anyone. But I would like to be a companion in the journey towards cozier games, and I think others would, too, if you would have us. It's difficult and slow and I'm probably asking a lot from you. But if you try and fall short of your expectations, please know that I will still support and celebrate you. I care about you, and your work is but a small part of what makes you wonderful. Good luck, if and when you're ready, – (your signature)

All in all, slow gaming seemed to be a part of the Zeitgeist, and my manifesto was just a humble and late addition to a wider trend. Although the conversation was still very niche, I felt the need for slower games was real.

My Collection of Slow Games

So it happened at the time I was co-running a small game studio called Different Tales with a friend, and we decided to put the slow game ideas to work.

The game we were working on, called *Wanderlust: Travel Stories*, was an interactive travel literature—a text-based simulator of the emotions you have when visiting new places and the memories that form on the way. It was also a journalistic perspective on the tourist industry. The characters were fictional but the places they visited were real, and the stories were weaved from real experiences—ours, those of the members of our team, or taken from reportages written by our journalist friends.

The writing was designed to be very immersive and intimate, written in the first person, and most of the choices concerned inner thoughts and emotional reactions to events, rather than fast action. Combined with journalistic photographs of the places visited and ambient music, *Wanderlust* was, without a doubt, a slow gaming experience. But it wasn't the only one, was it?

My own, very subjective collection of slow games looks like this:

- *Journey* (Thatgamecompany, 2012) is a short story about the cycle of life, loneliness, and the importance of human connection. It poses almost no challenge and lets you follow the path at your own pace.
- *Firewatch* (Campo Santo, 2016) explores the themes of friendship and loneliness while letting you explore the stunning vistas of a national park. The mystery you unravel is heartbreakingly down-to-earth at its core.
- *Stardew Valley* (ConcernedApe, 2016) is a farming life simulator where you can lose yourself in the rhythm of the seasons, and find pleasure in the smallest things.
- *The Longing* (Studio Seufz, 2020) tells a sad story of a shade waiting for his king to wake up while roaming a vast,

underground kingdom. It takes its time exploring loneliness, sadness, tragedy, and hope.

- *Unpacking* (Witch Beam, 2021) lets you into the private life of a protagonist you never see, but get the chance to intimately know, by unpacking her things after moving to new apartments.
- *Before Your Eyes* (GoodbyeWorld Games, 2021) is a game you play by blinking. It tells a story about looking back at your life. By making your body the controller it created one of the most moving moments I've experienced while playing games.
- *Disco Elysium* (ZA/UM, 2019) uses the tropes of a detective game to tell a deeply introspective story about failure, hope, and politics. For me, coming like the creators, from the post-soviet block, the visuals and metaphors were personally very moving.

At that time the COVID-19 pandemic was in full bloom, and during the lockdown, I decided to go back to the idea of slow games for the second time. I played them, I wrote about them, and I moderated slow gaming roundtables at industry conferences. The more I turned the ideas in my head, the more I felt the need to look critically at my initial manifesto.

Slow Burnout

The biggest problem I noticed was the postulate for sustainable development. I had no idea if the games I labeled, as a player or as slow games, were developed in a sustainable way. Moreover, from what I read, at least three of them—*Journey*, *Stardew Valley*, and *Disco Elysium*—were not. And frankly, even working at my own studio on games that we wanted to be "slow" ended with me severely burning out and withdrawing from the industry for almost a year.

Let's be realistic—I thought—a change that would introduce truly sustainable development would require more than a fancy manifesto. For such systematic changes to happen, you need some changes in the law, new government regulations, or at least unionization. I realized that my proposing a framework for the industry was an act of hubris more than anything else. Frankly, I had no idea what was good for the industry and it was not my place to guess.

My Second Take on Slow Games

Over those two years, I learned a lot about what was good for me as a creator. So, my second take on the Slow Gaming Manifesto took a much more personal turn.

Wholesome

I believe that there are more than enough games about bleak anti-utopias. Yes, we know that people can be cruel and selfish, and the world generally sucks. I want wholesome games that give me hope, inspiration, and present solutions rather than problems, helping me connect better with my humanity.

Organic

I believe that truth is important and it cannot be engineered but organically grows from the whole of our experiences. I want games that come to life to answer not the average market trends but the basic need to create. Games that were made by humans, not by human resources.

Local

I believe that there are enough games about saving the world and not enough about saving a moment. I want games that tell stories of people, places, and times that the mainstream overlooks; were made away from the main hubs of the game industry; and were inspired by things close to the creators, not to the non-existent average customer. I want to be exposed to ideas unknown to me and learn.

Sustainable

I believe that our main responsibility as creators is not to the market, not to shareholders, not to the company, not to gamers, and not even to the team—but to our creativity. I believe that our ideas and skills are the rarest of resources, and our responsibility is to keep them renewable. Pushing oneself to make a game may be OK. Burning out to make a game is never OK. I want games made by people who are allowed to take care of themselves and who work in a sustainable environment.

My Slow Gaming Manifesto

So, this is my second take on a Slow Gaming Manifesto—a design philosophy and an artistic path that I try to follow.

- I want a sustainable work ethic.
- I want local scope.
- I want organic inspiration.
- I want a wholesome message.

I believe that we can strive toward those values no matter what game we make and where we work. I believe that every step in the right direction is worth taking. If the path calls to you too, just start walking.

Looking Back

That was two years ago, as of the moment I'm writing this chapter. I feel it is a good time to revisit the ideas one more time.

From what I can tell, the idea of slow games didn't get traction—at least not under this name. People talk about cozy games, non-violent games, serious games, and games for change, and I feel that all of those terms strike similar notes. They play to the need for reflection, curiosity, peacefulness, real experiences, small and personal scope, and intimacy between the game and the player. I still think that a common name, a common tag on Steam, would help the discussion, but I can't say if I'm right. My game researcher friend once asked me why I use the name "slow games" to talk about what he saw as "artistic games." Maybe he was right.

There is another aspect of the slow movement worth mentioning. When we look back at where it all started—at the restaurant business—we notice how slow food became enmeshed with fine dining. Something that started as the appreciation of things and traditions local and organic became a part of an unsustainable, intense industry catering to the rich, who fly across the globe to eat overpriced local specialties. The owner of Noma, one of the most prestigious restaurants in the world, decided to close its doors, disillusioned with the movement he helped to create. The idea of slowing down turned out to be nothing more than a band-aid for the conscience of the elite.

I don't think that games are there yet, and I definitely don't want them to reach that point. Don't get me wrong—almost none of the players care about the conditions in which games are produced, and if they do care, they have no ways of influencing or changing the situation. Maybe it's better, more honest, if no big studio sees profit in offering high-priced "slow games" made by free-range developers.

Having said all that, I still see value in making games while taking good care of myself. I value telling small, personal stories, reaching for local scope, organically taking inspiration from everyday situations, and trying to convey a hopeful message.

I realize how personal it is: My needs and my values are by no means universal. Some of you may resonate with how I see making games, and many may not. I am OK with it.

Perhaps, in a few years, I will come back and try to label those quiet voices in the grand choir that is the game industry. Maybe I won't. For now, it is enough for me that those voices exist.

Notes

1 Published on itch.io by a Scottish game designer, Mitch Alexander. https://hxovax.itch.io/slow-games-movement-manifesto
2 https://www.projecthorseshoe.com/reports/featured/ph17r3.htm

11

GAMES OF THE END TIMES

MARTA FIJAK

The year is 2023, November. The Israeli attack on Palestine is in full swing. The Russian-Ukrainian war is reaching its second year. The world is on track for 2.5°C of global warming by the end of the century. New wealth, created since 2020*,[1] was in two-thirds gained by the richest 1%. Inflation has been on the rise, but wages stagnated in many places. Since the beginning of the year, 250,016 IT workers lost their jobs.[2] More than 8000* game developers who also lost their jobs were not counted in that number.*

Yet, with all of that is happening around us, I'm sitting here, writing about video games—little toys for humans, and at the same time, a market estimated to be almost 250 billion dollars.[3] A people-grinding, money-making monstrosity of a machine that at the end of the day brings people a way to kill their time*. In this book, I talk a lot about self-expression in games. This tension between games as products and as a way of communicating something

* 42 trillion dollars

* This number is not the full picture. Many companies do "silent layoffs"—just a few people every week—so it did not look like mass layoffs.

* This is just the tip of the iceberg of the current sorry show of reality. Let's not be a doomer though, for every one of those things created a strong opposite reaction—things like the Extinction Rebellion, Worker Unions' participation being on the rise, independent information sources fighting against propaganda, involvement in voluntary help to those affected, etc. I am not sure if this is enough, but it's a start.

* OK, also joy and many other good things, but please flow with this overly depressing tone for a moment.

 DOI: 10.1201/9781003325031-11

the creator finds important. Rarely do I talk about them as labor and a means to earn a living. Even this chapter, in the first draft, was called "Privilege of Expression in Late-Stage Capitalism." Is expression actually a privilege now*? It was never as easy as it is in the current day and age. Social media and, broader, Web 2.0* removed the gatekeeping of access to the masses. You do not need a contract with retailers to release a game*, you do not need a record label to release an album, you don't need a pub-lisher to put your book on Amazon, etc. In 2022, 6000[4] new games were released on Steam. That was 34 games a day. This year seems to have even bigger numbers. Expression is not a privilege—but in this oversaturated market of things fighting for our attention, being heard is a privilege.

* Remember that I am talking from a European perspective.

* The version of the Internet where the key aspect of a given web page is the content created by its users.

* Long time ago, you had contracts with physical stores to put your games on the shelf. Really.

Allegedly, 4 million songs on Spotify have never been played. No one listened to them even once.[5] Even if someone did, it would translate to $0.003–$0.005 per stream on average. So being heard but also making enough bucks to have a roof over your head, and a third monitor for coding, is challenging in this world of hyper-expression and rampant inflation is the privilege. Me and my co-author, Artur, are in this privileged position. We have more than 25 years of combined experience in devel-oping games*. Over that time, we both expressed ourselves through making games, but also made our living by doing that. Yes, games are, in a sense, a waste of time*. Yet year after year I want to think about them, make more of them, teach about them, and write about them. There are many reasons why. I wrote a whole chapter

* I'm writing it like this because, as with the wealth and 1%, Artur makes more than a half of the number, with his 17 years and my 10 years.

* Looking in an extremely utilitarian way, every cultural product is.

about it. Yet, how can I not be ashamed of my fascination when the world behind the window is ending?

There is the essay that I wrote in 2022, for the book *Homo Cyber Ludens*. It's called "Ludic Fulfillment." In it, I draw a possible future, in which real-world problems are beyond our comprehension. It's actually already happening. Those black boxes surround us from every side—from financial markets, through geopolitics, and ending on logistic chains. I do not mean that it requires specialized knowledge to understand them. I mean that those are complex systems that we can try to predict, like modern word divinations, but not "analyze" and "solve." This black box problem, with the rise of the new generation of AI, will only get bigger. Things happen because they do what they do, and we do not know why. Yet we need to solve problems, it is in our very nature. I draw a conclusion that maybe, in the future, the only way to scratch that itch would be in video games. Those artificial problems that game designers created for the players to solve, so after the fact, they felt smart. From that perspective, I can tell you that I do not feel ashamed about my game development path. I have a calling to create problems for you to solve. So you can feel fulfilled. I'm a supplier of ludic fulfillment. Yet, we, both you and I, know that this is bull.

I can also tell you that I see myself as one of the musicians of the *Titanic*. As the ship was sinking, they kept playing, to calm down the passengers and to make them feel safer in that unsafe moment. In the end, they all went down with the ship. Aren't we, the modern-day entertainers, the same? There is that quote from Karl Marx: "Religion is the opium of the people." Can we paraphrase it to "Entertainment is the opium for the people." The planet is slowly boiling, and social stratification is getting worse and worse. Here, we make something to numb everyone and keep people calm. A circus monkey at the end of the world, not ashamed of their role. Yet again, we both know that this is a horrible oversimplification and also not true.

So let's approach this shame from another perspective. Let's reframe this privileged position, and game fixation, as a means of transforming the world. I write about self-expression, so it seems to be crucial that I have something important to express. Yet what is worth expressing? What unique observation about the world or revealed truth do I have to share with the world? I'm a bloody toy maker. What important things do I have to say that will change the world? Can words even change the world? But I have to do what I do! I'm a creator! Again, there seems to be some doubtful shenanigans happening here.

Following all of those lines of thinking, it's easy to fall into despair, or even apathy. Curse this need for a higher purpose, significance, and global impact. We want to make games that not only make millions of dollars but also change the world. Why stop there? Save it! It would be great if they also cured cancer*. If not, then why even make them? Why make anything at all?

> * The only valid reason to crunch on a game is if it will save a life. Nothing else. My former lead used to tell me: "Go home; we are not curing cancer here."

There is the notion of the need for significance—this megalomaniac need for the whole world to be watching—but there is also another layer. We need to be the best version of ourselves. What does it mean? Success. And what defines success? Money and millions watching. It is as simple as that. So perhaps, to not be ashamed of what I do at the end of the world, I should strive for this monetary notion of success. Forget any deeper meaning—success is enough. A man a lot smarter than me explored this path—Byung-Chul Han. His book *The Burnout Society* explores this new form of control. We are controlling ourselves with this current paradigm of being the best version of ourselves—the most successful one*.

> * It is a horrible oversimplification of this book. Please read it—at least the first and the last essay.

Yet, I'm standing here, as the world is burning outside the window, and I'm not saving it with my games. I'm also not heard by millions, and I'm not making millions. Still, though, I am not ashamed. It might be a flaw of my character. Some undiagnosed psychopathology. Perhaps though, this is just OK.

There are few reasons that allow me to stand comfortably in the place where I stand. The first reason is that I deeply love games and what games do for people. There is nothing like the feeling when you see someone playing your game and their facial expression changes*—the brief sense

of wonder and engagement. You can't tell me that this is not enough. Players are not some mythical creatures that are separate from us, living in a magical land of a constant stream of numbing entertainment. They also have windows and can see what is happening. Frankly, many of them have a much better perspective than we have, because they are working in jobs that make them witness this sorry show up close and personal. Games offer a brief moment of relief. The space for social contact. A way to express themselves in our games, or a moment to forget about everything and recharge their batteries.

I know we've all already forgotten, but in 2020, all of us went under lockdown, as COVID-19 was killing millions of people*. Game sales skyrocketed. For

* Almost 7 million till today.

good reasons. They offered a safe way to spend time during the pandemic. *Animal Crossing* became a cultural phenomenon, selling more than 45 million copies. Many of us sought refuge on this small lovely island, and instead of discussing rising death counts, we discussed turnip prices with our friends. It was a blessing, disguised as a greedy raccoon that gave us a loan. Some people also sought both understanding but also gaining familiarity with the situation. We become less scared and more comfortable when we laugh or play with something we fear. A game released in 2012, *Plague Inc.,* suddenly became popular again. In this game, the player controls the diseases, trying to infect as much of the population as they can. So did the game, reaching 180 million players today. When there is an outbreak of a new disease, people start playing it again. They can see how plagues spread, and how vaccines and other measures stop their progress. They learn about it in this subversive way but also get more familiar with the topic, which lowers their anxiety.

Those are big examples, millions of players, but this magic of games also works on a small scale. I take part in game jams, mostly Ludum Dare. The games I make there are played by 200 people max. Yet when I watch the streams of them laughing while playing, I know I achieved something. That feels great.

The second reason is that games are a huge part of my life, but making games is not the whole of my life. The world is in a sorry state, and on a small scale, I can do something about it. Not as a developer, but as a human. I'm not saying that finding this balance is easy. We come to this industry out of pure passion. It can consume us to the bone. Yet, at the end of the day, this is a job. It's not our entirety. Every day, I strive to bring something worthwhile to the players. Yet, when the workday ends, I can interact with people in other ways. It does not have to be through games. I strongly believe it can also allow us to make better games. As, what can we tell about through our games, if we only know games? It sounds like a horrible cliche, but you need to live to create*.

* OK, you can also create a meta-game about game development. In that situation, you can skip this step. Yet, the world will still be burning outside the window. Just saying.

The third reason is that I'm not the main character. We already have enough of them. For many, I am probably an NPC, and I'm happy with it. Yet, I believe that telling those NPC stories can be important. There is a saying that when you create something personal enough, it becomes universal. We are all NPCs in a sense, but it does not mean we are not important. Being able to create something that other people can see themselves in is a superpower. It makes us feel less alone, and I find huge value in that, especially now.

The fourth reason is that I know there are a ton of things I won't ever understand, and that is OK. I'm trying to say that in this overconnected, overstimulated, and oversaturated world of content and short attention spans, things can still be beautiful and worthwhile, even if these are not "successful" or "curing cancer."

I teach students. Every year, there is a group of bright-eyed young people who just want to make games. They make many of them during their time in school, and 95% of them are student games. These games are not good from a "market perspective" in any sense, not going to make millions, and not going to be the next indie darling. Definitely not "curing cancer," but damn, how those young people are proud of them, beaming with confidence and wonder. They made a game! They should be proud; they started something, they finished it, and they poured all of their hearts into it. Then their family and friends played it, and they all felt something. Trust me, no one cheers as loud on student game jams as moms. I'm pretty sure that they are not entirely sure what is happening, but that does not matter. It's beautiful. If that's not worth something, then I don't know what is.

So I will keep doing what I do—not ashamed of it—to see the surprise on the faces of the players, and to see students make better and better games. But most importantly, I will keep doing all of these silly gamedev things for myself. It makes me happy. This profound waste of time—video games.

Notes

1 https://www.oxfam.org/en/press-releases/richest-1-bag-nearly-twice-much-wealth-rest-world-put-together-over-past-two-years
2 https://layoffs.fyi/
3 In 2022, it is estimated to be more than 600 in 2023. https://www.precedenceresearch.com/video-game-market
4 That's just the new games. There were 12,599 new items on Steam, but most of them were remasters, DLCs, definite editions, etc. https://steamdb.info/stats/releases/
5 https://www.cnet.com/tech/services-and-software/listen-to-the-4m-songs-never-played-on-spotify-with-forgotify/

Index

Printed in the United States
by Baker & Taylor Publisher Services